Discover...

- How to visit on a budget
- How to get the most out of your Zoo visit
- Most romantic places
- Suggested itineraries
- What's special for children
- Where to find the gardens

*To learn all this, and more...*see inside

Discover Balboa Park:

A Complete Guide to America's Greatest Urban Park

Second Edition

by Pam Crooks

Contributors:

Roger Conlee
Mary Anderson
Charlene Baldridge
Susan Bernstein

House of Hospitality Association

Ridgway Park Publishing
San Diego, California

Second Edition

Art director: Laurie Berg
Cover photographer: Brett Shoaf
Printing: RanRoy Printing, San Diego, California

Library of Congress Catalog Card Number: 2006940369

ISBN 0-9706219-5-7

Although the author, contributors and publisher have made every effort
to ensure the accuracy and completeness of the information contained in
this book, we assume no responsibility for errors, inaccuracies, omissions,
or any inconsistency herein. We welcome comments, suggestions
or corrections for possible use in future editions.

Write to us:
Ridgway Park Publishing, 666 Upas St., #1202, San Diego, CA 92103

E-mail: editor@balboaparkguide.com

www.balboaparkguide.com

Would you like to help preserve Balboa Park?

The San Diego Foundation currently manages the only
significant endowment specifically designed to preserve
Balboa Park for future generations—**Forever Park**.
For further information on making a donation to the endowment
or creating your own fund to benefit Balboa Park in a
loved one's memory, to honor a special person
or just in gratitude for time spent in the Park,
call (619) 235-2300 or log onto **www.foreverpark.org**.

*Dedicated to the memory
of two long-time Balboa Park friends,
Inge Dickens and Robert McGlade*

Preface

Although there haven't been any dramatic changes to the buildings and grounds in Balboa Park since the first edition of this book was published in 2000, there has been a great deal of activity behind the scenes in the cultural institutions. Several Tony Awards were given to plays that premiered at The Old Globe Theatre; the National Science Foundation has funded significant permanent exhibitions at two of the museums, the San Diego Zoo welcomed two new panda babies since the last edition of this book was published and the San Diego Lyric Opera has left the Park for its own home in the old North Park Theater. Better connections with downtown and San Diego Bay were created when the new Petco Park baseball stadium was built and soon rapid transit buses will connect the ballpark, Balboa Park and downtown to points north and east by way of Park Blvd.

Downtown San Diego has changed as more and more people are choosing an urban lifestyle. That means these new residents can take full advantage of all the wonderful offerings seven days a week in Balboa Park. I'm one of those lucky people. My husband and I just moved to a condo near the Park and are enjoying life here just as much as we thought we would. I've recently joined one of the International Cottages volunteer groups and hosted a Sunday open house, participated in a 5K walk in the Park, ridden a bicycle to the annual Ethnic Food Faire, and walked to the Zoo. My husband jogs every morning here.

Once again, as I edit this new edition I'm overlooking downtown and Balboa Park. Only this time I'm more invested in its continued success. It's now become our home. I'm thrilled to share it with you, my readers.

Pam Crooks

Table of Contents

Welcome to Balboa Park!

INTRODUCTION

There is no place on Earth like Balboa Park. History, art, architecture and green-space, all contribute to its magic. Called the "Smithsonian of the West" because of the close proximity of its 15 museums, it is so much more.

An outstanding collection of museums, theaters, performing arts venues and one of the world's finest Zoological parks entertain and educate millions of visitors each year. A multitude of recreational opportunities may also be found in this splendid setting. Here the visitor can explore formal lawn bowling and hiking trails...folk-dancing and jazz ballet...award-winning Shakespeare and the world's largest motion pictures. Everything from hands-on science and serious art to puppetry and pandas exist side by side with a recreation center for the blind and a disc (Frisbee®) golf course.

The first thing you will notice when you arrive is the balance between romantic architecture, graceful trees, flowers, fountains and people. You will also notice the cleanliness and freshness of the well-traveled public areas. This level of care speaks more eloquently than anything else about how the Park came to be. Early citizens created and preserved it. Today dedicated San Diegans continue to protect it, donate to it, volunteer in it, vote for it, and use it!

A visit doesn't have to be expensive–in fact a whole day can be spent without laying out much cash at all. For less than you would spend at Disneyland for the day, you can experience most of the Park's cultural attractions–if you have the stamina for it! But it's also possible to enjoy the gorgeous outdoor environment and recreational offerings without spending more than the cost of the gas to get there and maybe a picnic lunch.

These days there is an admission charge for almost all major museums around the world. It's just not possible for municipalities to cover the large cost of operating a fine museum with tax money. It only makes sense to "tax" those who enjoy its contents. Balboa Park's museums are no different. But they do make their wonderful collections available free one weekday each month (with a few exceptions), and in most cases at a greatly reduced cost to students on field trips.

And what a wonderful experience this is for young students. Where else in the world can one study ancient human artifacts, some of the rarest animals in the world and take in an award-winning play all in one day?

Balboa Park is the largest urban cultural park in the United States, maintaining its unique position as a place not only to exercise the body, but the mind and soul as well. Much like Europe, part of the magic happens just by getting out of your car and walking. There is a deep satisfaction that arises from slowing down and connecting with your surroundings in this way. This is what Balboa Park is all about.

CHAPTER 1
HOW BALBOA PARK CAME TO BE

with contributions by Roger Conlee

In the late 1800s, the City of San Diego was little more than a dusty burg at the southwestern corner of the U.S. Most of the city was still located in the area we now call Old Town. But a few entrepreneurial spirits such as Alonzo Horton saw the potential for another site about a mile or so south, closer to the waterfront– an area soon known as "New Town." This new area was quickly subdivided, and growth began in earnest.

Perhaps this calculated move from one part of town to another, or the careful planning that went into the subdivision of the lots in New Town, gave this group of leaders more foresight than they might otherwise have had. Maybe they wanted to ensure that private development of the City didn't completely cover all of the nearby surrounding hills and mesas. Or maybe it was a move to contain the outward growth, and encourage development closer to the waterfront. But in 1868, these leaders set

Cabrillo Canyon, circa 1903

aside a 1,400-acre parcel on a scrub-filled mesa overlooking New Town, and declared this public parkland.

When those early San Diegans looked up toward their new "City Park" from New Town, they probably didn't imagine lacy mounds of eucalyptus trees and fairytale towers, but they had a vision nonetheless. Most of them migrated to this area from elsewhere and appreciated San Diego's fine climate and natural beauty.

The area looked much like the undeveloped hills and mesas look today, rising from the Pacific as you drive north on Interstate 5 through the Camp Pendleton Marine Corps Base; there was very little vegetation–mostly sagebrush with few trees–but commanding views. You can get a glimpse of the original pristine nature of the area if you drive or hike through Florida Canyon where the native vegetation and wildlife still flourishes in Balboa Park.

This is how the Park remained for over 20 years, although there were moves from time to time to encroach on it. The State of California officially recognized it in 1870 as parkland. But almost as quickly, some entrepreneurial types tried to get legislation passed in Sacramento to free up some of the land for commercial development. Fortunately this movement was stopped in time, and only city-sanctioned use continued.

The impact of Kate Sessions

Limited planting of trees started in 1889, but didn't begin in earnest until an enterprising young woman from San Francisco made a deal with the City. In 1892, in exchange for 32 acres of land in the northwest corner of the Park for her commercial nursery, Kate Sessions offered to plant 100 trees a year within the Park as well as donate 300 trees and shrubs for use elsewhere in the City.

Seeds were imported from all over the world for this purpose. Hundreds of exotic and fast-growing trees began to dot the landscape. Trees native to Australia, Spain, Mexico and South Africa, such as eucalyptus, pepper, cypress and acacia, were favored. Because she studied and sought trees and shrubs that would succeed in our semi-arid climate, many of them still flourish today. She also recognized the exceptional beauty of the

Park's natural site, and discouraged attempts to fill in the canyons to create artificial lakes, or to plant trees and other foliage that required a great deal of water. In 1902 she supported creation of a formal Park Improvement Committee, and the hiring of a professional landscape architect to guide the Park's development. Samuel Parsons, a well-known landscape consultant for New York City parks, was retained to develop a plan in San Diego that would later lead others to call Balboa Park the most beautiful park in the nation.

Ultimately a very distinctive landscape, unlike any other city park in the country, evolved. Many of the original trees still exist today, thanks to Kate Sessions' knowledge of horticulture. She insisted that the young trees be planted properly in large enough holes to allow the roots to flourish in the hardpan soil. The dirt was so unyielding in some cases that holes had to be blasted to successfully plant the trees.

...distinctive landscape, unlike any other city park in the country, evolved

She maintained her nursery in Balboa Park until 1903, when landscaping work on the Park began to affect her nursery business. After that time she continued to lead formal and informal efforts to beautify the Park. In March 1904, she organized the first of many annual Arbor Day celebrations (in the Park) when hundreds of citizens and school children gathered to plant trees and shrubbery on barren hillsides overlooking the canyon area now bisected by Highway 163.

During her long life, Kate Sessions left her mark throughout this City by landscaping other important civic sites and homes of prominent San Diegans, but she is best known as the "Mother of Balboa Park," a name she was officially given during the California Pacific International Exposition in 1935. She helped found the San Diego Floral Association—an organization that still meets regularly in the Park. Many scholarly articles and essays she wrote about her travels and botanical discoveries can be found in archival issues of the association's monthly journal—the oldest gardening magazine in California.

From 1903 on, planting continued, irrigation systems were installed, and roads built. The Park began to look very different. Originally known as "City Park," the name was changed to "Balboa Park" in 1910–the result of a winning entry in a citywide naming contest. The name honors Vasco Nuñez de Balboa, the European explorer who first sighted the Pacific Ocean (although from the coast of Panama not California). Today, beautiful views of the Pacific are still enjoyed from several high points in the Park.

The first international exposition

The Panama-California Exposition provided the impetus for the Park's first major thrust toward what it is today. Celebrating the completion of the Panama Canal, the Exposition was held in 1915 and extended through 1916. Planners said the Exposition's purpose was "to illustrate the progress and possibility of the human race," and a vast array of exhibits were designed to both educate and entertain.

The Expo opened on New Year's Eve, December 31, 1914. At exactly midnight San Diego time (3 a.m. in Washington, D.C.), President Woodrow Wilson pressed a telegraph key in the White House. That impulse zipped to Balboa Park and turned the lights on all over the Park. Seconds later, Army artillerymen fired shells into the sky, 7,000 red flares ignited, and a Navy cruiser in the bay flashed on its powerful searchlights. The Expo was open in a blaze of light!

Appropriately, the amusement zone was called "The Isthmus." Almost a mile long, the fun zone was placed in what is now the San Diego Zoo's parking lot. The Isthmus featured a working model of

the Panama Canal; Chinese, Japanese, Hawaiian and Mexican villages; a model gem mine; candy factory; live animals (including an ostrich farm); games; concessions, and a 6,000-foot roller coaster billed as the world's longest.

The first female stunt pilot ever to do "loop-de-loop" turns, Kathleen Stinson excited crowds at the 1915 Expo, sometimes even performing at night with flares on the end of her wings.

Well-known publisher William Randolph Hearst brought the Liberty Bell to Balboa Park. Hearst paid to have the American icon shipped from Philadelphia and displayed at the fair in November 1915.

The Foreign & Domestic Arts Building (now the House of Hospitality) was one of many buildings created, primarily in the Spanish Colonial style, for the Exposition.

Others included the Spreckels Organ Pavilion, Botanical Building, Commerce and Industry Building (Casa de Balboa), Varied Industries (Casa del Prado) and the Indian Arts Building (now the House of Charm).

Occupying the southwest corner of Plaza de Panama, the Expo's main quad, the future House of Charm was inspired by the Basilica de Guadalupe in Guadalajara, Mexico. A display of 10,000 tiny lights that looked like fireflies illuminated Montezuma (now Alcazar) Garden, just behind the building. Built in Hartford, Conn., for the Exposition in 1915, the Spreckels Organ is still considered the world's largest outdoor organ.

...the Spreckels Organ is still considered the world's largest outdoor organ

The Cabrillo Bridge-California Tower complex awed visitors entering the Expo's west gate. Besides the 1,500-foot-long bridge, the complex includes the California Building with its signature tower and distinctive Moorish-tiled dome. Two deep archways across El Prado connect the building's north and south wings.

Today's Park-goer is surprised to learn the California Tower and Building (Museum of Man) were one of very few structures designed to remain permanently in the Park. The others were temporary wood-and-plaster structures scheduled to be torn down after the fair.

Hail to the Chiefs

Former and future presidents came to the fair. Theodore Roosevelt delivered a speech on the steps of the Sacramento Valley Building (current site of the Museum of Art) on July 27, 1915, and on September 16, William Howard Taft spoke at the Spreckels Organ Pavilion.

Future President Franklin D. Roosevelt, then assistant secretary of the Navy, watched his boss, Navy Secretary Josephus Daniels, dedicate Cabrillo Bridge on April 12, 1914. FDR and Daniels were the first to cross the bridge. FDR would return as president in the 1930s and during World War II, when San Diego played a dominant role as a major naval base. President Franklin and First Lady Eleanor Roosevelt visited the House of Hospitality on October 2, 1935. Former President Herbert Hoover also visited the Park in 1935.

The Zoo's beginnings

In the Expo's second year, the official surgeon of the fair, Dr. Harry Wegeforth, launched the fledgling San Diego Zoo. The idea supposedly came to him when the roar of a caged lion displayed at the Expo impressed him. Wegeforth became the Zoo's first president, a position he held until his death in 1941, long after his project grew to become one of the world's finest zoos. As did Kate Sessions, Harry Wegeforth brought back exotic plant specimens and seeds from his world travels in the early years, transforming the Zoo grounds into a paradise of plants as well as animals.

A fight to save the buildings

The military took over most of the buildings after the Panama-California Exposition. Throughout the 1920s, public debate raged over what to do with the remaining structures, which reverted to civilian use after World War I. By the early 1930s, the roofs leaked and walls flaked, and mass demolitions were proposed. Shocked at such sacrilege, a citizens committee led by Gertrude Gilbert raised money to save the buildings.

> By the early 1930s, the roofs leaked and walls flaked... a citizens committee raised money to save the buildings.

Meanwhile, on the night of November 25, 1925, the Fireman's Ball at the former Southern California Counties Building was sadly and ironically canceled because the building caught fire. On-duty firemen, as well as those decked out in black-tie for the ball, battled in vain to save the structure, then known as the Civic Auditorium. After the fire, the site was cleared and the San Diego Natural History Museum opened there in 1933, in a building designed by architect William Templeton Johnson.

Impact of the Great Depression

Several of today's best-known Park features emerged during the Depression years. Now a Balboa Park landmark, the 23-foot statue of the legendary Spanish warrior El Cid Campeador, (Rodrigo Diaz de Vivar) was unveiled in the plaza in front of the House of Hospitality in 1930. The Anna Hyatt Huntington sculpture depicts El Cid astride a gallant stallion. Besides the advent of the Natural History Museum at the east end of El Prado in 1933, on the Park's East Mesa, a crude golf course with sand greens, nicknamed the "Rock Pile," was upgraded to an all-turf, 18-hole course in the same year. Golfers today still enjoy the Balboa Municipal Course, perched above Florida Canyon.

Another expo is proposed

To help dispel the Depression doldrums and inspired by Chicago's 1933-34 World's Fair, "Century of Progress," San Diego decided to host a second major fair in the Park in 1935-36, called the **California Pacific International Exposition**. Because of the Depression, few San Diego companies had money to contribute, so a grassroots fund drive was launched. The goal: $500,000. Schoolchildren literally gave pennies out of their lunch money. Amazingly, citizens eventually raised $700,000.

By early 1935 the money was in place, along with federal WPA (Works Progress Administration) funds to build new buildings and upgrade old ones. It took several thousand men working around the clock to open the Expo on time. They put up a host of new buildings (including six large structures in the Palisades area, the Spanish Village complex, and fifteen House of Pacific Relations cottages) in less than 12 months—an enormous construction accomplishment unimaginable today.

Many of its exhibits having been shipped directly from the Chicago World's Fair, the California Pacific Expo opened on schedule, May 29, 1935.

Park changes for a new expo

The new fair's principal architect, Richard S. Requa, designed buildings both inspired by the native architecture of the Southwest and Central America and that of Renaissance Spain and Portugal. These buildings, along with those constructed for the 1915 Expo, present appealing examples of pre-Hispanic, Spanish Colonial, and Mission Revival architecture. Requa's firm redesigned the interior of the House of Hospitality, facing Plaza de Panama, in time for the second expo. He patterned the courtyard of the remodeled House on a museum in Guadalajara, Mexico. "Woman of Tehuantepec," the distinctive Donal Hord sculpture of a seated Mayan woman, was added to the courtyard at that time.

Most of the buildings in the Park's southern Palisades area (called Pan American Plaza today) were produced for this fair. They include the Ford Building and adjacent Ford Bowl, today known as the San Diego Air and Space Museum and Starlight Bowl. Built by Ford Motor Company to house a living demonstration of how cars were built, the Ford Building reflected the latest in design and technology at the time. Ford Bowl, with its excellent acoustics, hosted outdoor musical performances during the Expo.

In 1936, the fair's second year, the Ford Building was restyled as the Palace of Transportation. The *March of Transportation* murals that still adorn the walls of the Air and Space Museum were painted at that time by a Hollywood set designer, Juan Larrinaga and his assistants.

Also erected for the 1935-36 fair (and still in existence today) were the Women's Palace (Palisades Building, home of the Marie Hitchcock Puppet Theater), the California State Building (Automotive Museum), Federal Building (Hall of Champions Sports Museum), Palace of Electricity and Varied Industries (Municipal Gymnasium), the Christian Science Exhibit Hall (United Nations Building) and the Old Globe Theatre (reconstructed in the late 1970s). The original Old Globe building built for the fair was a replica of the 16th Century Globe Theatre on the Thames River in Elizabethan London. Many other buildings from the 1915 Expo were renovated for the 1935-36 event.

The Expo featured a gold mining camp. Besides a simulated mine, "Gold Gulch" had a dance hall, saloon, sheriff's office,

shooting gallery, Chinese laundry and a bank with iron-barred windows. The camp occupied a ravine west of today's Reuben H. Fleet Science Center still known as Gold Gulch Canyon. More notorious was the nudist colony in Zoro Gardens, located just east of today's Casa de Balboa. It was an adults-only attraction, but San Diego boys quickly found all the knotholes in the surrounding fence.

The fair ended in September 1936, and visitors began entering Balboa Park for free again. On the East Mesa, a municipal pool and, later, ball diamonds and a velodrome for bicycle racing, enhanced the area named for longtime Park superintendent John Morley. By 1941, tennis courts were also built in the Park's northeast corner—now known as Morley Field Sports Complex.

The Park goes to war

During World War II, most of the buildings on the Central Mesa were taken over by the Navy as extensions of Balboa Naval Hospital. Museum exhibits were moved out, hospital beds moved in. More than 400 beds were placed in the Museum of Art, while the House of Hospitality became a nurses' dormitory. The Army occupied Spanish Village and operated an anti-aircraft battery in the Sixth Avenue area.

One of the Park's most photographed features, the 257-foot-long reflecting pond in front of the Botanical Building, made a splash with wounded sailors — they used it as a rehab pool. With the war winding down in the summer of 1945, the pool was opened to the children of San Diego.

The carillon, whose resonant chimes peal out across the Park every quarter hour, was installed in the California Tower and first played on Christmas Day, 1946.

> More than 400 beds were placed in the Museum of Art, while the House of Hospitality became a nurses' dormitory.

Broadway versus Boeing

In 1948, Starlight Opera began performing Broadway musicals in the former Ford Bowl. The acoustics remained excellent until the jet age brought noisy interruptions from planes approaching Lindbergh Field. Starlight briefly moved to Wegeforth Bowl in the Zoo, and then the outdoor theater at San Diego State. But tradition-minded San Diegans, who loved to picnic on Park lawns before the shows, urged a return to Starlight Bowl.

Encroachments

Originally a near-perfect 1,400-acre square, Balboa Park has been whittled down to 1,170 acres, its edges chipped away for various purposes. The establishment of Russ School (now San Diego High) shaved off one parcel in 1882. North of the Zoo, Theodore Roosevelt Junior High School stripped off seventeen acres in 1922. In 1948, a large lily pond was wiped out when the controversial Cabrillo Freeway cut a four-lane swath through the Park, in order to connect downtown and Mission Valley. Park lovers have energetically blocked all subsequent efforts to widen the freeway with additional lanes.

At least grass and trees framing Cabrillo Freeway offer one of the most beautiful approaches to downtown San Diego. Another major encroachment occurred in the early 1960s when the eight-lane Interstate 5 freeway lopped off the Park's southwest corner with no such niceties.

While patriotic San Diego is proud of its military heritage, not everyone favored construction of a new naval hospital in the Park. The original Balboa Naval Hospital was built in 1922 on a hilltop north of San Diego High School. Its distinctive pink buildings were often featured on-camera by NBC when the San Diego Chargers played in nearby Balboa Stadium.

These buildings gave way to a modern hospital in Florida Canyon in the early 1980s after heated local debate. The new hospital takes up many acres of otherwise pristine Florida Canyon, just west of the Park's Central Mesa. Today only three of the old hospital buildings remain: a chapel, now serving as the Veteran's Museum and Memorial Center; the original 1922 hospital building now housing administrative offices of the San Diego Park and Recreation Department; and a more modern medical library building.

Earthquake, fire, and growth

The Timken Museum, an architectural anomaly in Balboa Park, opened on Plaza de Panama in 1965. Designed by Frank L. Hope, the Postwar Modernist style Timken is clad in Italian marble. After an earthquake in 1968 caused major damage to the original structure, the former Food & Beverage Building was rebuilt and

reopened as the Casa del Prado in 1971. The Reuben H. Fleet Space Theater and Science Center, named for San Diego aircraft manufacturing pioneer Reuben H. Fleet, made its debut two years later.

In 1978, tragedy struck the Park twice within a two-week span. On February 22, fire swept through the San Diego Aerospace Museum, then located in the Electric Building (today known as the Casa de Balboa) on the Prado, destroying the entire collection, including a flyable replica of Charles Lindbergh's "Spirit of St. Louis." Two weeks later, flames gutted the Old Globe Theatre, the Shakespearean treasure from the 1935-36 fair.

Private and public support was rallied, enabling both institutions to continue. The Aerospace Museum (today's Air and Space Museum) moved into the renovated Ford Building in the south Palisades area, and the Old Globe was rebuilt on its same site. A temporary outdoor theater was rushed into existence beneath eucalyptus trees in an adjacent canyon to accommodate the Globe's 1978 summer season. It has since been upgraded and made permanent as the Lowell Davies Festival Stage.

The Casa de Balboa was constructed on the site of the old Electric Building and opened in 1981, as the new home of the Museum of San Diego History, San Diego Hall of Champions, Museum of Photographic Arts (MoPA), Balboa Art Conservation Center, and the San Diego Model Railroad Museum.

The San Diego Automotive Museum took over the former Conference Building in the Palisades area, opening in 1988, two years before the Japanese Friendship Garden emerged between the House of Hospitality and the Organ Pavilion.

A statue of "Mother of Balboa Park" Kate Sessions was dedicated in the Sixth Avenue area of the West Mesa in 1998; nearby statues of three other Park advocates were erected in 1999. The Federal Building, in the Palisades area became a new, much larger home of the Hall of Champions in 1999, while MoPA expanded to fill the space they vacated in the Casa de Balboa in 2000.

The Park and Recreation Department

A third larger than New York City's 864-acre Central Park, Balboa Park is managed by the City of San Diego's Park and Recreation Department. Since 1989, the City has been involved in a major way in renovating and restoring the buildings and grounds, upgrading the lighting, and improving public access.

Two major examples of historic replication commissioned by the city are the House of Charm and the House of Hospitality. No longer safe or up to code, they were razed and reconstructed during the 1990s. Rebuilding of the House of Charm was completed in 1996, and the building became host to the Mingei International Museum and the San Diego Art Institute/Museum of the Living Artist. As a registered National Historic Landmark, the House of Hospitality was replicated in a $15 million City of San Diego project, winning many prestigious awards for its meticulous historic reconstruction. Completed in 1997, the interior appears as it did during the 1935-36 Exposition, while the exterior looks the same as it did during the 1915 Panama-California Exposition.

On to the 21st Century

Expansion and renovation of the San Diego Natural History Museum were completed in 2000 and include a new modern entry and north facade. While Balboa Park hasn't hosted a world exposition since 1936, it was designated as the official site of San Diego's millennium celebration, **Exposition 2000**. Festivities took place in the Park for three days beginning December 31, 1999, with follow-on activities over the next twelve months.

The City's Park and Recreation Department staff plants the gardens, maintains the grounds, administers a year-round program of recreational and cultural activities within Balboa Park, provides the free trams and Park Ranger program and coordinates numerous annual Park events, including December Nights and the Earth Fair in April. A recently formed Balboa Park Cultural Partnership represents the interests of the museums, performing arts and other cultural groups within Balboa Park. Several private non-profit organizations such as The San Diego Foundation's Balboa Park Advisory Board, Legler Benbough Foundation, Committee of 100, Friends of Balboa Park and Patrons of the Prado provide funds for special projects and serve as "watchdogs" for the public's interest.

> **Hint:** For more in-depth information on the entire history of Balboa Park, there is a great Web site, **www.sandiegohistory.org/balboapk.htm** and a wonderful book on the subject: **Balboa Park: A Millennium History** by Roger Showley. For more about the contributions of Kate Sessions, be sure to read **Kate Sessions: Horticultural Pioneer** by Elizabeth MacPhail or the charming children's book **Kate Sessions: Mother of Balboa Park** by Joy Raab. These, and other books relating to Balboa Park's history, are available at the Balboa Park Visitors Center or at the Museum of San Diego History Store.

Planning Your Visit

CHAPTER 2
BEFORE YOU GO–THE BASICS

For the most enjoyable experience in Balboa Park, start with a little advance planning. Ask yourself several questions before you go. How much time do you have? Are you interested mainly in the history, architecture, or cultural aspects of the Park?

Maybe you prefer to stroll around just taking in the scenery, a free concert or street entertainers. If you're a photography buff you need to know the best spots to take those prize photos. If you're into hiking, biking or in-line skating you need to know where you can safely enjoy these activities. By doing some quick research, you'll be able to see and do almost everything you wish to, and prevent wasted time getting there and parking, or discovering that the one exhibit you most wanted to see just closed.

Waters Café at Museum of Art

Good places to get current info

A good place to start is by picking up a local newspaper on a Thursday. *The San Diego Union-Tribune's* **"Night & Day"** pullout section on Thursdays usually has a section on Balboa Park, including current offerings at the museums and theaters. *The San Diego Reader*, a freebie, which also comes out on Thursdays has a good listing of current events and activities that include Balboa Park museums and theaters. Both of these are readily available throughout the county. In the Park, there is a *Union-Tribune* newspaper dispenser at the eastern edge of the Plaza de Panama next to a post office box. The *Reader* may be picked up at the Japanese Friendship Garden's Tea Pavilion.

> It's important to have a current listing of activities since the exhibitions, plays and concerts change frequently

It's important to have a current listing of activities since the exhibitions, plays and concerts change frequently. Without even leaving home or your office you can also access the following Web sites on the Park. **Particularly recommended is the Balboa Park Web site maintained by the House of Hospitality: www.balboapark.org.** Since the staff also publishes the Balboa Park Events Guide, a handy brochure that is updated every other month, their information is the most reliable. You will also find links on this site to most of the cultural organizations in the Park.

Best Web sites on Balboa Park:

www.balboapark.org
www.signonsandiego.com
www.sandiego.gov/park-and-recreation/parks/balboa.shtml

NOTE: *Use of a good search engine will bring up several other Web sites on Balboa Park, but their information is not as complete as the sites listed above, nor are they kept current.*

You can also **call the Balboa Park Visitors Center** for specific information, **(619) 239-0512.** The center's phones are staffed by knowledgeable volunteers, many of whom have "worked" in the Park for years. The Visitors Center is located in the House of Hospitality on the Plaza de Panama (the central plaza in the Park), and is open from 9:00 a.m. to 4:30 p.m. daily, with extended hours in the summer.

> *The Balboa Park Visitors Center*
> *c/o The House of Hospitality*
> *1549 El Prado, Balboa Park*
> *San Diego, CA   92101*
> *(619) 239-0512*

Getting there

Balboa Park is conveniently located next to downtown San Diego. Just a short (10 minute) taxi ride from the **San Diego airport at Lindbergh Field**, the **San Diego Convention Center**, the **B Street Cruise Ship Terminal**, or any of the hotels in downtown, **Mission Valley**, and on **Harbor** or **Shelter Islands**. The Park is also no more than a 10-15 minute ride from the **Marine Corps Recruit Depot**, **Old Town**, or **Coronado**—less than a $12 cab ride from most of these locations! It's about 20 minutes by car from most of the **beach areas**, **UCSD**, **32nd Street Naval Station**, **Miramar Marine Corps Air Station**, and the **northern**, **southern** and **eastern** suburbs. The **border with Mexico** to the south, and **Camp Pendleton (U. S. Marine Corps training camp)** to the north, are both about 35-45 minutes away depending on traffic.

Once you've decided how you want to spend your day, take a little time to plan your route and parking. Parking is quite limited so this advance planning can save you driving around in circles and many extra steps at the end of a long day of sight-seeing.

Don't rule out public transportation, which is actually quite convenient. Those of us in Southern California don't think of mass transit as the first option, but would be wise to consider it— particularly if one has good access to **the San Diego Trolley** or **public bus route #7**, which **runs frequently right through the Park** on the east side. A ride on the red San Diego Trolley can deposit you at City College— about a 15-minute walk from the heart of the Park. Or catch a ride on bus #7 across the street from where the trolley drops you off, and ride up Park Blvd., for no additional cost (if you show your trolley ticket).

Entering the Park

There are two ways to approach the cultural heart of the Park–from the east side along Park Blvd., or from the west along Sixth Avenue. The most scenic and historic original entrance to the Park is from the west on Laurel Street. This will take you across Cabrillo Bridge with its heart-stopping views of the California Tower, archways and fountains that have become the icons of the City. Try to enter from this direction if at all possible for your first introduction to the Park.

However, the quickest way to access parking and public transit is to travel along Park Blvd., from the north or the south.

Time of day is important

If you're planning a visit during the week, it's advisable to wait until after 9 a.m. to hit the freeways. Most of the Park attractions don't open until 9:30, so have an extra cup of coffee and relax. If you're an early riser who enjoys the outdoors, you should get there around 7 or 7:30 in the morning. You'll see many San Diegans running or walking their dogs through the Park at this hour. The morning light and fresh air are wonderful. If you're not in a hurry, take in one of the garden spots mentioned in Chapter

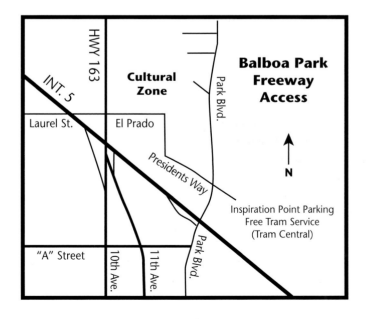

3, and ask a gardener a question or two about your favorite plants. Of course this is also a great time to take pictures (see section on best photo spots).

> **NOTE:** *If you're visiting early...you're not allowed to park on the street before 9 a.m., and a few of the smaller parking lots do not allow parking before 8:30 a.m.; the Parking policy varies from lot to lot. Check all signs before leaving your car early in the morning!*

To access the Park from Park Blvd. (the East side):

Heading south on Interstate 5 (from Los Angeles, Pacific Beach, La Jolla, Del Mar, etc.), take Highway 163 North/10th Avenue Exit and bear to your right on 10th Avenue. Go two blocks to A Street and turn left. Go two more blocks and turn left again onto Park Boulevard. At the second stop light, which is President's Way, you can make a choice to go left into the heart of the Park and look for parking there, or turn right into two large lots that are in front of the Balboa Park Administration Bldg. (**Inspiration Point parking lots**). Pick up free tram service into the heart of the Park from here (but be sure to read the caveat on page 33).

Heading north on Interstate 5 (from the international border, Chula Vista and other South Bay communities), take the **Pershing Drive exit** and follow the signs to the San Diego Zoo and Museums. You will turn left onto Florida Drive at a major intersection in Florida Canyon. Go past the entrance to the Naval Hospital and turn left on Zoo Place. At the lights at the top of the hill you will be facing the entrance to the San Diego Zoo.

If you don't wish to park at the Zoo (which is a bit of a hike from the central area of the Park), turn left on Park Blvd. at this intersection. You will see parking lots on the right as you head down Park Boulevard. You could turn right into one of these, or keep heading south to the third stoplight at President's Way. Turn right towards the heart of the Park and take your chances on parking, or turn left into the two large lots below the Balboa Park Administration Building. There you can pick up a free tram into the center of the Park (see below).

On Interstate 8 going east or west, or from Interstate 805 going south, take **Highway 163 South** through the heart of Balboa

Park. Watch for the **Park Boulevard/Interstate 5 North South Exit**. Follow the signs carefully! This is a two-part off ramp and provides a tricky exit to Park Boulevard. Head off Highway 163 to the right but stay in the left lane heading towards the Interstate 5 South on-ramp. Almost immediately you will need to get over to the right to exit on Park; otherwise you will find yourself headed south towards South Bay and the Mexican border!*

At the end of the off-ramp, turn left on Park Boulevard. About two blocks north you will find yourself at the intersection of President's Way and Park Boulevard. Head either left into the heart of the Park, looking for parking or right into the two large lots in front of the Balboa Park Administration Building (former Naval Hospital headquarters). There you can pick up the tram service mentioned below. If you continue north on Park Boulevard, at the third light you will reach the San Diego Zoo entrance. This will be a left-hand turn into the Zoo parking lot.

> **NOTE:** *Many a surprised tourist has tried to make a dangerous switch to the right after they found themselves in the left lane headed onto I-5 South—better to just head south to the first available exit to turn around. If this happens, just exit, get back on Interstate 5 heading north, and follow the directions given above for reaching the Park from Interstate 5 North.*

To access the Park from Laurel Street (west side):

There are two easy ways to do this **from Interstate 5**. **If you're heading south on I-5** take the **Sassafras Street exit**, drive a few blocks south on Kettner, past Sassafras, to Laurel. Turn left and head up the big hill towards Balboa Park. This will take you right into Balboa Park. (But don't try this if you are a new driver on a standard shift car! This is one of the steepest hills in San Diego.) Or **from Interstate 5 North or South**, take the **Highway 163 North exit. From Highway 163**, take the **Quince Street** exit. This will bring you out on the west side of the Park. At the end of the curvy, steep off-ramp, turn left at the stop sign, which is Balboa Drive. Go straight ahead to Laurel Street, and turn left. Go across the bridge into the heart of the Park. You won't find much parking in the central plaza, but the view and feeling you get entering the Park from this direction are worth it.

Follow the signs for the one-way traffic flow towards the Organ Pavilion; in fact, your best bet for parking is behind the Organ Pavilion, which you'll pass on your left. If parking is not available here or any of the other lots you see nearby, turn left at President's Way. Go straight across Park Blvd. into the large lots in front of the Balboa Park Administration Bldg. where you'll be able to pick up the free tram.

It is also possible to easily access the West side of the Park **from Interstate 8 East or West** by taking **Highway 163 South** and exiting quickly on **University Avenue**. Stay in the center lane on this off ramp, and you will be heading directly south on Sixth Avenue towards Balboa Park. Although there are a number of stoplights going this direction, traffic flows quickly and easily, and you will be at Laurel Street in no time. The streets in this area are named for trees, which appear in reverse order alphabetically in this direction. Watch for Laurel once you pass Palm. It's only three more blocks.

Parking tips

Parking in Balboa Park is almost always a challenge unless you know where to look. As mentioned above, you can usually find parking in the lots off Park Boulevard, in front of the Park Administration building, with free tram service into the heart of the Park. But if you prefer to park closer to the heart of the Park, check behind the Organ Pavilion first—easily accessed from either approach to the Park (President's Way or Laurel Street). The best feature of this lot is easy access to the Prado as well as the Palisades (Pan American Plaza) and International Cottages area.

The lots behind the Fleet Center and the Natural History Museum, both accessed off Park Boulevard, are good bets if you plan to explore the museums at the east end of the Prado, Spanish Village, or the Rose/Desert Garden–but they fill up quickly. Park Boulevard has free parallel parking available on both sides of the street after 9 a.m. The Zoo lot and the carousel lot also serve this side of the Park, but the Zoo lot fills early on busy days.

The Palisades lot in front of the Air and Space and Automotive Museums is huge and is a good bet when visiting only this end of the Park. However, it's about a 10-15 minute walk from here to the Natural History Museum, Casa del Prado, or Spanish Village.

There are small lots behind the Casa de Balboa building, Botanical Building and Alcazar Gardens, but these are almost always full with staff vehicles. Unless you have a handicapped placard in your windshield don't even bother looking in these or the Plaza de Panama (main plaza with the small fountain in front of the Museum of Art and the House of Hospitality). You may get lucky if you arrive very early, but after 9 a.m., it's usually a waste of time to circle and search for a spot in this area.

Disabled parking

There are multiple spaces available in the Plaza de Panama as well as pedestrian drop off areas. Parking lots throughout the Park have designated spaces for this purpose, and almost all of the attractions have pedestrian drop off areas available for guests. Most importantly, pay attention to signage and park in designated areas only!

THREE NOTES OF CAUTION: *(1) If you're visiting early…several of the Parking areas do not allow parking before 9:00 a.m.; this varies from lot to lot. Before leaving your vehicle check the signs on the light poles for the posted hours! Parking enforcement staff have given many a ticket even five minutes before the official restricted hours end. (2) Always park within the white or yellow lines for your parking spot. Parking citations are sometimes given for tires parked outside the lines! (3) Lock your car and place any valuables out of sight or in the trunk. If you have a "club" or other anti-theft device, use it. While the Park is generally a very safe place to visit, car prowls and thefts occasionally do pose a problem. As in any big city, use common sense when it comes to protecting your personal property.*

Free tram service

Catch a free red tram (looks like an old-fashioned street car on wheels) that runs from the lot by the Balboa Park Administration Building at Inspiration Point approximately every 10-15 minutes, to the heart of the Park in front of the Timken Museum of Art in the Plaza de Panama, with one other stop along the way. To hop on and off the tram, you must wait at one of the designated tram stops. The tram runs every day from 10 a.m. to 6:30 p.m., with extended service and extra trams during daylight savings hours and on holidays. Small folding wheelchairs and strollers may be brought on board. Most trams also have wheelchair lifts.

A knowledgeable driver will point out the sights to you. If you have time, you can even ride across the Laurel Street (Cabrillo) bridge and back, as the tram makes a loop every half-hour (on the top of the hour and then again on the half-hour) in this direction. This will give you a sense of the more historic, formal entrance to the Park intended by the original planners. This is a good option for almost anyone who wishes to avoid the parking hassles, and have a good overview of what the Park has to offer.

It's also possible to get on and off the tram when you tire of walking. For instance, if you want to walk back across the Cabrillo Bridge but it seems like too much of a hike to do it both ways, you could take the tram across and walk back, or vice versa.

NOTE: *Be sure to check the signs at your tram stop and/or ask the driver when the last pick-up will be in the interior of the Park, and where. The hours of the tram service may be extended in the near future, but the tram type and even the route may be different than that described above.*

Old Town Trolley service

Many first time visitors arrive in Balboa Park on an Old Town Trolley, which offers a pleasant historic bus tour of the city. Open air "trolleys" drive in a continuous loop around central San Diego, making stops at eight popular locations, including two in Balboa Park. Passengers are conveniently picked up at any one of the locations and may get on and off the trolley until they return to their original boarding point.

With careful planning, the Old Town Trolley makes it possible for a visitor with limited time in San Diego, to explore other parts of the City in combination with a visit to Balboa Park—all in one day!

Along the way the Old Town Trolley ride is narrated by trained guides and is quite informative. The two stops in Balboa Park are: El Prado at the House of Hospitality/Balboa Park Visitors Center, and the San Diego Zoo. Tickets may be purchased in the Visitors Center. The trolley stops at each location approximately every half hour throughout the day.

Drop offs and pick-ups begin in front of the Timken Museum at 10:05 a.m., and run every half-hour until 4:35 p.m. (5:35 p.m. during peak summer season). The cost runs around $30; half that for kids. Inquire at the Visitors Center, check out the Old Town Trolley Web Site, **www.historictours.com**, or call (619) 298-8687.

Safety in the Park

Balboa Park is probably the safest, most well-used urban park in the country.

Balboa Park is probably the safest, most well-used urban park in the country. It is estimated that as many as 14 million people use the Park every year. Park security falls under the jurisdiction of several different groups, including the San Diego Police Department, San Diego Park and Recreation Department's Park Rangers, and the R.S.V.P. (retired senior volunteer patrol). You may see a mounted police officer on horseback chatting with people. Park Rangers lead walking tours and there is a **Community Relations Police Storefront Office** located in the House of Hospitality, near the Visitor Center. If you have a problem, let someone in the Storefront or the Visitors Center know, or notify a Park Ranger or museum staff member.

While crime is not something a visitor should anticipate, it pays to use common sense when visiting any unfamiliar area. Stay in the public areas if you are alone, especially at night. Park in lighted areas. If you attend a lecture or theater performance at night, walk with someone to your car. Most of the institutions that have evening programs have staff that will be happy to escort you. Just ask.

There are many wonderful walking trails and off-the-beaten paths you can take to experience a different view of the Park. But just as in any large City, it's probably not a good idea to go off into remote areas by yourself. Take a friend! It's more fun that way anyway.

You may occasionally run into a homeless person, but these encounters are rare and generally harmless. Statistically, violent crime is negligible; more concerning to the visitor are car prowls and break-ins, and even these have been on the decline recently. Of course if it happens to you, it can be very unsettling and disruptive to your holiday.

Food options inside the Park

Eating out in Balboa Park is a fun experience, whether you're just enjoying an ice cream cone from a concession stand, or a gourmet salad in an upscale restaurant. This, and everything in between, is available depending on your mood and pocketbook.

Full/limited service restaurants:

The best-known restaurant in Balboa Park is **The Prado** located in the historic House of Hospitality across the courtyard from the Visitors Center. Operated by a highly-regarded San Diego restaurant partnership, this very attractive venue should be a must on anyone's list of places to eat in San Diego. Besides a menu featuring Mediterranean entrees including Spanish and Italian cuisine, there are local favorites such as Baja-style fish tacos, and plenty of vegetarian entrees.

If the wait for a table is long (mainly on weekends and holidays), ask for seating in the bar. Just as atmospheric, the full-service bar offers a smaller menu with hearty appetizers and light meal items and features a happy hour with discounted prices from 4-6 p.m. and 8 p.m. to closing Tuesday through Friday.

Outdoor seating is available on the terraces overlooking the Casa del Rey Moro Gardens and its wishing well–one of the most popular wedding sites in the city. The atmosphere of the historic House of Hospitality, recreating the elegant style of the 1935 Exposition, is very special not only for weddings, but for other important private and corporate events. They can accommodate group sizes from 30 to 1500. For lunch or dinner reservations at The Prado, call (619) 557-9441; for House of Hospitality wedding or banquet information, call (619) 232-9333.

Lunch at **The Prado** is an occasion in itself, but if you are on a budget or rushed for time, another option for upscale (but very reasonably priced) dining is close by. **Waters Café @ SDMA**, situated adjacent to the San Diego Museum of Art in a modern outdoor sculpture garden, is a good choice for a gourmet lunch. You order from an interesting menu of freshly made soups, salads and sandwiches at the entrance and a waiter delivers the food to your table. They do not offer full bar service, but do serve wine and beer. Be aware that Waters is closed on Mondays and is open primarily for lunch, but features one of the nicest locations in the heart of the Park to enjoy a meal. For Waters Café information, call (619) 237-0675.

> Tobey's 19th Hole... is the only place within the Park where you can get a full cooked-to-order breakfast.

If you don't mind a bit of a hike and the price of a Zoo admission (members receive free admission), another option within the Park for a full-service restaurant is **Albert's**, located in the Gorilla Tropics area at the San Diego Zoo. They offer a wide range of entrees, including a children's menu, and the option of dining in a tropical garden setting. Reservations may be made at Albert's and are recommended during peak season. Ask for a table by a window or on the small deck overlooking the waterfall. You'll swear you're in an exotic tropical locale! Call (619) 685-3200.

There is one more restaurant offering table service—at the **Balboa Park Golf Course**. Called **Tobey's 19th Hole**, it opens daily at 6 a.m., and is the only place within the Park where you can get a full cooked-to-order breakfast. They are known for their tasty hamburgers, and have a lovely view towards downtown, overlooking the 18th fairway. The grill caters mainly to golfers, with very reasonable prices. However, don't expect much in the way of atmosphere—the aging clubhouse and restaurant are scheduled for renovation in the near future. Open each day 6 a.m. until dusk. Call (619) 234-5921.

Fast-food options:

Beyond these four sit-down options, there are several fast food places to choose from within the Park. **The Village Grill**, on the corner of Village Place, next to the Casa del Prado Theater, serves hotdogs, hamburgers, soup, chicken quesadillas, nachos, soft-serve ice cream, drinks and other traditional park fare. Good-sized concrete tables with umbrellas are available nearby, or stroll through Spanish Village Art Center while you nosh. Open daily from 9 a.m. to 5 p.m.; until 6 p.m. in the summer, (619) 702-2428.

Galileo's Cafe located next to the fountain plaza at the Reuben H. Fleet Science Center, offers a healthful alternative to traditional fast food. The menu includes soups, salads, pizzas, vegetarian sandwiches, fruit juices, gourmet teas and flavored coffees. A good choice for families with small children; however seating is limited. Pick up items and enjoy them sitting on the edge of the fountain or on the shady lawn nearby. Open daily from 9:00 a.m. until the building closes, normally 5 p.m. or later. (619) 238-1233 x 829.

The Café in the Park is a cozy place tucked away in the lobby of the Casa de Balboa (near the Museum of San Diego History, the Museum of Photographic Arts, and the Model Railroad Museum). It offers muffins and croissants, made-to-order sandwiches, espresso drinks, and soft drinks. Open Mon., 9 to 2:30 p.m.; Tues. - Fri. until 4 p.m.; Sat. & Sun., until 4:30 p.m., (619) 237-0322.

Lady Carolyn's Pub at the Old Globe Theatre is an outdoor food and beverage pavilion, which opens one hour before curtain time during Theatre season. Afternoon service is available before and during matinee performances on weekends. It offers soups, salads, desserts, British ales, wine, fruit juices and specialty coffees. The pub, which also offers mixed drinks, is open to anyone, but the idea is to arrive early, avoid the parking hassles, and enjoy a light picnic supper prior to a performance. For other info, call (619) 231-1941 x 2751.

Two good choices south of El Prado include the **Tea Pavilion** at the Japanese Friendship Garden, and the **Time Out Cafe** at the San Diego Hall of Champions. The **Tea Pavilion**, (619) 231-0048, offers sushi, soba noodle salads, rice bowls and teas and rice cookies in a soothing environment, while the **Time Out Cafe**, (619) 702-6240, makes deli sandwiches to order, has hand-dipped ice cream and ice-cold beer, sporting-event style.

Also available in the Palisades area near the Air and Space Museum and Starlight Bowl is a snack bar offering hot dogs, nachos, candy bars, popcorn and sodas, open 10–5 p.m. daily and just prior and during **Starlight Musical Theater** performances.

On peak days you can usually pick up a hot dog, pretzel, hand-dipped ice cream bars, frozen lemonade and the like at one of the snack carts on the main thoroughfares. **Daniel's**, a cappuccino cart inside the House of Hospitality Courtyard offers hot and cold espresso drinks and pastries daily until 4:30 p.m.. These quick-service carts close up shop around 4-4:30 when most of the museums close, so gauge your hunger pangs accordingly. (Or proceed to the Fleet Center's Galileo's Café, open later than most other quick food service in the Park.)

Food options outside the Park

Since the above-mentioned food service options within the Park can't possibly accommodate everyone visiting Balboa Park, here's a short list of alternative places within easy driving distance of the Park (no more than five to 10 minutes drive in any direction). One or two are even within reasonable walking or jogging distance. Parking is usually easy to obtain unless otherwise stated.

For those who prefer to have a pleasant, full-service meal before or after your visit to the Park, there are many good choices in the vicinity. Not surprisingly some of San Diego's most enduring restaurants, with a loyal Park-related clientele, are located in this area.

Full-service restaurants near the Park (by area)
West side:
- **Bertrands at Mr. A's** – 2250 Fifth Ave., (619) 239-1377. Offers gorgeous views of the downtown skyline, the bay and sunsets from the top of the Fifth Avenue Financial Center. The owners also operate one of the most highly respected restaurants in the region (Mille Fleurs in Rancho Santa Fe). Expect excellent food and service. Open for lunch Monday - Friday, dinner daily. $$$$

- **Laurel** – 505 Laurel Street, (619) 239-2222. Upscale setting very close to Park entrance at 5th & Laurel. Trendy Asian fusion menu. Open daily, but only in the evenings. $$$
- **Mandarin House** – 2604 Fifth Ave., (619) 232-1101. Tradtional Chinese menu, attractive, comfortable decor. Yummy lunch specials. Open for lunch Monday - Friday, dinner daily. $$
- **Gemelli's** – 495 Laurel St., (619) 234-1050. A welcome addition to the west side of the Park since the construction of many high-end condos in the area, Gemelli's is a classy Italian trattoria owned by one of the leading restaurant operators in San Diego. Open for lunch and dinner. Offers Sicilian favorites as well as more exotic takes on classic Italian dishes. $$$
- **Top of the Park** — 525 Spruce St. (619) 291-0999 For a delightful lunch with a rooftop view of Balboa Park, try Top of the Park restaurant at the Park Manor Suites Hotel. Recently remodeled, this light and bright space has a menu to match at reasonable prices. With the construction of several high-rise condominiums in the area, this is one of the last places you can dine overlooking the Park's west side. Open for lunch from 11:30 to 2 p.m., Monday through Friday only. $$
- **Hob Nob Hill** – 2271 First Ave., (619) 239-8176. The ultimate breakfast place; also very good for lunch and dinner. Comfort food. May experience a wait, especially for breakfast, but it will be worth it! A San Diego favorite since 1944. Open daily. $$
- **Imperial House** – 505 Kalmia, (619) 234-3525. Across the street from the Park. Traditional decor and menu with lovely Park views through multi-paned windows. Big comfy chairs and booths. Open in this great location since 1969. Lunch served Monday - Friday, dinner Tuesday through Saturday only. $$

Northeast side:

There are dozens of restaurants in the area north of Balboa Park along Park Boulevard and University Avenue. Just a few favorites are mentioned here.

- **Terra** – 1270 Cleveland Ave. #K, (619) 293-7088. Conveniently located with plenty of free parking in the Uptown District shopping center (Cleveland and University Ave.). Terra offers a relaxed setting, good wine list and seasonal menu. Open for lunch and dinner daily and brunch on weekends. Terra even features a Doggy Menu and dog-friendly patio seating. $$
- **Cafe on Park** – 3831 Park Blvd., (619) 293-7275. Popular with Park employees, this tiny place has eclectic decor, excellent food and friendly service. Limited seating capacity. Open daily for breakfast & lunch. Dinner Tuesday – Saturday only. $
- **Parkhouse Eatery** – 4574 Park Blvd., (619) 295-7275. Although located a bit further away, north along Park Boulevard in University Heights, this is another popular destination with Park insiders. Charming cottage atmosphere, outdoor patio, very creative menu. Open for daily breakfast, lunch & dinner. $$

East side:

- **The Big Kitchen** – 3003 Grape St., (619) 234-5789. Community gathering place "where the body is nourished along with the soul." Sumptuous breakfast platters, homemade soups, chili and desserts. Many items for the vegetarian or health conscious members of your party. Be prepared for a long wait on the weekends—it's worth it! $
- **Turf Supper Club** — 1116 25th St., (619) 234-6363. A fun place to go (for those 21 and older) after a day on the Balboa Park Golf Course links or museum-hopping along El Prado, this 50s-style bar and restaurant wasn't designed to be retro—it's the real thing. Sip the latest martini concoctions while you grill your own steaks, swordfish kabobs or Portobello mushrooms. Open evenings only. Noisy, popular hangout with a twenty-something crowd after 9 p.m. Arrive early and stake out a table. $$

- **Vagabond Restaurant** — 2310 30th St., (619) 255-1035 A relatively new destination in trendy South Park, Vagabond: "Kitchen of the World," features a full bar, international menu and wine list, romantic décor and candlelight. Only seats 40, so gets very crowded on weekends, but if you manage to get a reservation or visit on a weeknight, you won't be disappointed. $$$

Fast-food options near the Park

An assortment of popular food places offering a wide variety of carry-out cuisine for any occasion can all be found within a mile or so of the Park entrances. All are open for lunch and most are available for take-out picnic suppers as well. Please remember that take out food comes with mega-packaging. Be considerate and dispose of or remove all trash when you leave. Recycle bottles and cans. Bright blue recycling bins are located throughout the public areas of Balboa Park.

- **Grant's Marketplace and Delicatessen** – 2953 Beech St., (619) 231-0524. Delicious breakfast and lunch items to go. Order a custom-made sandwich or one of their specialty salads and head to the Cedar Street Tot Lot or Bird Park for a breezy picnic! Open daily 6:30 to 9 p.m. $
- **Marketplace Deli** – 2601 Fifth Ave., (619) 239-8361. Convenient place to pick-up good deli sandwiches, drinks, chips and other munchies for a picnic in the Park. (Also a free copy of *The Reader* on Thursdays with its guide to "Events & Attractions," including many activities in Balboa Park.) Very convenient to the west side entrance of the Park on Laurel.
- **La Salsa** – 1010 University Ave., (619) 543-0777. For the freshest, healthiest Mexican food around, look for this convenient, friendly take-out place on University Avenue in the Uptown District shopping center. Great vegetarian burritos, Mexican salads, and delicious hand-prepared salsas.
- **Pick Up Stix** – 1040 University Ave., (619) 295-7849. Not your parents' Chinese food, this stuff is prepared with no MSG, and only lean meats and crunchy fresh vegetables. You can watch as your favorite dishes are prepared. Also

conveniently located in the Uptown District in Hillcrest, north of the Park.

- **European Market & Deli** – 4135 Park Blvd., (619) 298-8661. Featuring Middle European and Middle Eastern cuisine; conveniently located on Park Blvd. in the same block as Henry's Market (large fresh produce and health food store). Enjoy the Old World ambience of the sidewalk cafe or pack a picnic for a Sunday afternoon in and around the International Cottages in the heart of the Park.

- **McDonald's** – For those grown-ups who have to have a "Big Mac" or have finicky kids who yearn for the familiar comforts of home, never fear, there is a McDonald's close by. Two locations in fact. One at 1414 University Ave., (619) 298-8968, north of the Park on University Ave. (near Park Blvd. and University Ave. intersection) and another at the other end of Park Blvd., 1260 12th Ave., (619) 234-4700, near City College. Just head south on Park Boulevard towards downtown—you can't miss it on the right hand side about 1/4 mile south of President's Way.

- **Trader Joe's** – 1092 University Ave., (619) 296-3122. Planning a gourmet picnic, complete with wine, breads and cheeses? They have pre-made entrees, sushi and sandwiches to go. Located in the Uptown District shopping center in Hillcrest, right next to Ralph's grocery store (where you can find anything else you might need).

- **Henry's Market** – 4175 Park Blvd., (619) 291-8287. Similar to Trader Joe's but with more of an emphasis on health food, fresh produce and vitamins. Henry's also has ready-made entrees, good bread, herbal teas, and an ATM. Pick up beautiful fruit in season, inexpensive trail mix and bottled water for that Park Ranger-guided walking tour in the heart of the Park. Situated on the east side of Park Blvd. about a mile north of Upas.

- ...And the closest **Starbucks**, if you must know, is located on the west side near the intersection of Fifth Avenue and Laurel Street (El Prado becomes Laurel Street after you cross Cabrillo Bridge heading west).

Of special note...

- **Extraordinary Desserts** – 2929 Fifth Ave., (619) 294-7001. We're talking romance and decadence here. This is a wonderful place to go with the one you love after an Old Globe or Starlight Theatre performance. Or pick up one of their signature creations to conclude a fabulous picnic supper at the Organ Pavilion prior to a Summer Twilight Concert. This might necessitate adding candles and fresh flowers however. You can find Extraordinary Desserts on Fifth Avenue near Quince Street.

> **Hint:** For the same fabulous desserts, plus other breakfast, lunch and light supper items, visit Extraordinary Desserts' new restaurant on Union St., in Little Italy. There you will find a much larger space with a modern art museum feel.

Restroom/baby changing facilities

The most centrally located facilities are at the **House of Hospitality near the Balboa Park Visitor Center**, but you will also find clean, well-lighted rest rooms in each of the museums and public buildings throughout the Park. The more modern the building the more up-to-date the facilities, including better wheelchair accessibility.

Most of the museums reserve their facilities for their visitors, but a few offer some near the front entrance that you can use. For example the **Reuben H. Fleet Science Center** and the **Museum of San Diego History** each have restrooms with changing facilities near the entrance that you can use without purchasing an admission. The Fleet also has pop-down diaper changing units in the men's restrooms as well as the ladies' and at least one is equipped with a diaper machine. **The Zoo also provides clean, comfortable facilities** for nursing and changing babies (but you must have an admission ticket or be a member to get inside).

Spanish Village north of the Natural History Museum has public restrooms as does the **Casa del Prado building** located at the corner of Village Place and El Prado. These do not have good baby changing facilities.

If you're in the **Pan American Plaza** area near the puppet theater and the international cottages, **try the Balboa Park Club** building. It's usually open on weekdays, and often on weekends when events are planned there. They have beautifully clean, lighted restrooms located off a peaceful foyer. The **Hall of Champions** also has bright, well-tended bathrooms **near the Time Out Cafe.**

The restroom facilities **closest to the Spreckels Organ Pavilion** are a step up from the usual **outdoor public facilities.** Also available, but not very comfortable, are the **public restrooms adjacent to Alcazar Garden** (near the Archery Range), **adjacent to the Air and Space and Automotive Museums,** on the Sixth Avenue side **near the Redwood Club, on Balboa Drive near Marston Point,** and in **Pepper Grove picnic area adjacent to the Parking lot.** These are standard concrete bunkers—no mirrors, cold water, limited-toilet-paper facilities, but of course will do in a pinch. Similar restrooms are available at **Morley Field near Bird Park,** at the **Disc Golf Course,** the **Golden Hill Area** and **Grape Street Park** on the East Side.

Bike and Rollerblade®/skate rentals

Balboa Park is a great place to take a bike ride, and this is a good way to cover a lot of territory if you're mainly interested in its outdoor attributes. With the exception of Spanish Village, the Rose Garden, Botanical Building, Desert Garden, and the House of Pacific Relations, there are no restrictions on where you can ride bicycles in the Park as long as you stay on the roads and bicycle paths and avoid the sidewalks. Bicyclists under 18 must wear helmets in California.

If you wish to visit the Zoo, one of the museums or sit down restaurants, you can lock your bicycle to one of the few available bike racks, but be sure you have a state-of-the-art lock. Sophisticated bike thieves sometimes target the racks in Balboa Park, although this problem has been on the decline recently. Better to be safe than sorry!

Three **convenient bike rack locations** in the central core include the Reuben Fleet Science Center on the north side of the building; the Botanical Building near the bridge over the Lily Pond; and near the sidewalk in front of the Japanese Friendship Garden.

The closest rental place is located downtown on Fifth Avenue. However they will deliver and pick up bikes in Balboa Park. Rent by the hour or the day for very reasonable rates. Call **Bike Tours San Diego**, (619) 238-2444.

Many people enjoy in-line skating, skateboarding and roller skating in Balboa Park, but these activities are only permitted west of the Cabrillo (Laurel Street) Bridge, in the area of Sixth Avenue, and east of Park Boulevard. **No skating of any kind is not allowed anywhere between the bridge and Park Boulevard in the Central Mesa area. Skating is also not allowed in the Desert Garden, Rose Garden or in Bird Park. Park Rangers can, and do, issue tickets for offenders.**

The closest skate rental place is downtown in the Gaslamp Quarter. Rentals may be obtained by the hour, 1/2 day or all day. Their rates are quite reasonable. **Rent-A-Skate** is located at 523 Island Avenue; call (619) 595-0211.

There is a **lengthy expanse of the Park**, which is quite pleasant for skating or bike riding, south **along Balboa Drive from Upas to the area known as Marston Point**. Be aware that since this is a city street which loops around on one end–you'll be sharing the road with cars. But what you'll see are picnickers, sunbathers, volleyball, lawn bowling and horseshoe games in progress, spreading shade trees and lawn areas, squirrels, and unusual views of the city and the bay that most visitors to the Park never see.

> There is a lengthy expanse of the Park, which is quite pleasant for skating or bike riding, south along Balboa Drive from Upas to the area known as Marston Point.

This area is a popular gathering place for the gay and lesbian community of nearby Hillcrest, and the site of the Gay Pride Parade and Festival every summer.

Places to stay near the Park

Balboa Park is easily accessible from just about any hotel location in San Diego by taxi, car, Old Town Trolley or bus service. **Mission Valley** and **Downtown** are the **two closest areas** with a concentration of full-service, "name-brand" hotels.

Mission Valley tends to be less expensive and **more family-oriented**, while downtown hotel properties are generally more expensive and conventioneer-oriented. But these are both centrally located areas, about a **10-minute car or taxi drive** from the Park's attractions. **Old Town** and **Little Italy** are two other areas with several hotel offerings that are fairly close—a 10-15 minute drive.

Places to stay in the actual **vicinity of the Park** are increasing. Three now are within easy walking distance.

- **The Balboa Park Inn** — located at the northeast corner of the Park on Upas and Park Boulevard, about two blocks north of the Zoo, is a sparkling clean and comfortable place, with a knowledgeable, friendly staff. Featuring 26 suites with names like Greystoke, Casa de Oro, and Nouveau Ritz, the decor is quite flamboyant, but fun. Address: 3402 Park Boulevard; phone: (619) 298-0823. Fax: (619) 294-8181. For reservations, (800) 938-8181. Web site: **www.balboaparkinn.com**

- **Britt-Scripps Inn** – A gorgeous Victorian boutique hotel (really a glorified bed and breakfast) on the corner of Fourth and Maple is a recent addition on the west side. Built in 1887, the inn has been carefully restored and furnished to the period. There are nine rooms, each with private bath, including a separate cottage that has its own porch. Address: 406 Maple St.; phone: (619) 230-1991. Fax: (619) 230-1188. For reservations: (888) 881-1991. Web site: **www.brittscripps.com**

- **Keating House Bed and Breakfast** — Another restored Victorian that requires walking a bit further than the Britt-Scripps Inn, but is less expensive, Keating House is located in Bankers Hill near Second Ave and Juniper intersection. Address: 2331 Second Avenue; (619) 239-8585. Web site: **www.keatinghouse.com**

Hint: A stay in one of these bed and breakfast places, dinner at The Prado Restaurant along with tickets to the Old Globe Theatre one evening, followed by "Best of Balboa Park" Passports and a guided or self-guided walking tour the next day, offers the ultimate Balboa Park experience in the author's opinion.

- **Park Manor Suites** is an historic high-rise also on the west side of the Park, at the corner of Spruce and Sixth, dating back to 1926 (some rooms, halls and public areas are currently undergoing some renovation). They offer spacious suites, some with nice views of the Park. Junior suites and one- and two-bedroom suites are available for nightly, weekly or extended stay rates. Perfect for families. There are two restaurants on-site—one downstairs that is open for dinner only, the other upstairs on the top floor, is a lovely space for continental breakfast and lunch. Or visit a local favorite across the street—**Jimmy Carter's Restaurant** (619) 295-2070. Hotel Info…address: 525 Spruce St.; phone: (800) 874-2649 or (619) 291-0999; fax: (619) 291-8844 Web site: **www.parkmanorsuites.com**

- **Best Western Cabrillo Garden Inn** on Cortez Hill is just a quick bus ride (Bus route #7) or a 20-minute walk from the heart of Balboa Park. This small, charmingly renovated motel near City College, Petco Park and Symphony Hall has been getting very positive reviews from travelers. Address: 840 A St.; Phone: (866) 363-8388 or (619) 234-8477; Web site: **www.bestwestern.com**

> **Hint:** Best Western Cabrillo Garden Inn is also conveniently located near a main station for the San Diego Trolley, which can take you (a transfer may be needed) anywhere on its route, whether it be downtown to the Gaslamp Quarter, Santa Fe train station and the waterfront; the Mexican border or Old Town State Historic Park.

- **Inn Suites Lafayette** on El Cajon Boulevard, near Park Boulevard, is a popular spot with families and seniors. Hotel shuttle transports guests back and forth to the Zoo entrance. This older, remodeled hotel has a history with a Hollywood connection; in fact the huge swimming pool in the center courtyard was designed by Johnny Weismuller of Tarzan fame. **(Note that part of this hotel will be under construction for at least two years, starting**

in 2006. **During that time the pool may not be available.)**
Rates are reasonable, decor is tasteful, and rooms are
spacious. Continental breakfast is included. Many full-
service restaurants are within walking distance. For an
inexpensive meal (open for breakfast, lunch and dinner)
in a cheery, coffee-shop atmosphere, try **Johnny's Family
Restaurant** just four blocks east at 2611 El Cajon Blvd., (619)
291-8239. InnSuites info…address: 2223 El Cajon Blvd.;
phone: (800) 842-4242 or (619) 296-2101; fax: (619) 296-0512.
Web site: **www.innsuites.com/hotelsandiego.html**

> **Hint:** For an inexpensive European-style hostelry,
> try La Pensione in Little Italy. Great location
> between Balboa Park and the bay in a colorful
> neighborhood of art galleries and great restaurants.
> (619) 232-3400.

Taking your dog to the Park

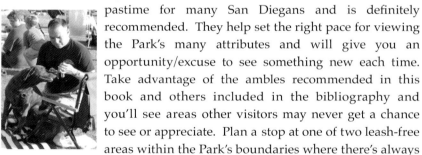

Walking canine friends in Balboa Park has become a favorite
pastime for many San Diegans and is definitely
recommended. They help set the right pace for viewing
the Park's many attributes and will give you an
opportunity/excuse to see something new each time.
Take advantage of the ambles recommended in this
book and others included in the bibliography and
you'll see areas other visitors may never get a chance
to see or appreciate. Plan a stop at one of two leash-free
areas within the Park's boundaries where there's always
plenty of canine-loving company and you may even make a new
friend or two of the human kind.

The two 24-hour leash-free zones are: 1) **Nates Point** at the
intersection of Balboa Drive at El Prado on the south side of the
Laurel Street entrance to the Cabrillo Bridge; and 2) across Florida
Canyon at **Morley Field** on the northwest side of the tennis courts.
There is a third leash-free area at **Grape Street Park in Golden
Hill**, but the hours are limited.

In these areas it is your responsibility to keep your pet
under control at all times and within the posted boundaries of

the "Designated Dog Off Leash areas. It is a violation to allow your dog to run free to these areas from the Parking lot. Released only within the leash-free boundaries, your dog will be protected from rattlesnakes, traffic and other hazards or distractions, while having a large open space to run free, play fetch and socialize with other dogs.

Just a few guidelines will help you enjoy your visit with your dog(s). Keep him on a leash not to exceed eight feet. This includes trails and canyons in all the Parks throughout San Diego. Remember that Balboa Park is a very busy pedestrian area. This rule protects pedestrians, bicyclists, and other dogs from being chased and/or bitten. Municipal code also requires that your dog be licensed and that you clean up after him. **Heed the signs as violators will be cited!**

Good places to rest

Sitting and people-watching or day-dreaming are a requisite part of any visit to the Park. There are many good places to kick back and relax in addition to the restaurants or food stations already mentioned, where you can linger over a coffee after your meal and watch the action. It really depends on what you're looking for.

Here are a few ideas within each quadrant of the cultural zone of the Park. Some are sunny spots, some shady. Each has many benches available, and restrooms close by. Most are good places to let kids run around while you keep an eye on them. (More ideas on this in a later chapter.) A few have water features and others may offer glimpses of street entertainers.

South quadrant:
- Courtyard in center of International Cottages
- Lawn area near Balboa Park Club (at President's Way)
- Benches in front of the Federal Building (Hall of Champions Sports Museum)

Central core:
- Organ Pavilion and curved porticos
- Alcazar Garden
- House of Hospitality courtyard
- Around the Lily Pond
- Any shaded arcade (covered walkways along El Prado)

West quadrant:
- Shade garden behind Museum of Man
- Sefton Plaza/Lawn Bowling Court
- Playground on Sixth Avenue near the Redwood Club

East quadrant:
- Around the Bea Evenson fountain at the Plaza de Balboa.
- Near Moreton Bay Fig ("Big Fig") tree north of the Natural History Museum
- Spanish Village courtyard
- Rose Garden

Good meeting places

There is so much to see and do in Balboa Park that your group may choose to split up to enjoy different activities. Here are some recommended spots to meet near several easily-found Park landmarks.

- **El Cid** – the statue on the Plaza de Panama between the House of Hospitality and the House of Charm
- **House of Hospitality courtyard** – peaceful retreat from the crowds; near the Visitors Center
- **Lily Pond** – in front of the Botanical Building; lots of benches; good place for people-watching.
- **Sefton Plaza** (entrance to Laurel Street entrance/Cabrillo Bridge) – best meeting place on the west side
- **Bea Evenson Fountain** – between the Natural History Museum and the Reuben H. Fleet Science Center on the Plaza de Balboa; lots of places to sit; rest and people watch.
- **Moreton Bay Fig** ("Big Fig") tree – north of the Natural History Museum; near main food concession stand, walkway to the Zoo and Spanish Village Art Center.

Disabled access/services

Access for the disabled in the Park has greatly improved in the last few years as the original buildings have been reconstructed and refurbished. Staff from San Diego Park & Recreation Department have worked closely with a disabled services advisory group to gradually bring older buildings into compliance with ADA guidelines.

Every parking lot has spaces for disabled visitors and convenient drop off locations, but recently many more parking spaces have been added for the disabled in the most convenient locations, especially in the Plaza de Panama between the House of Hospitality and the House of Charm. The free Park trams, which pick up and drop off visitors in this plaza, have added wheelchair lifts.

Ramps have been added at the Organ Pavilion; handrails on the steps lead up to the big fountain at the Plaza de Balboa. Almost all bathrooms are wheelchair accessible with the best facilities available in the most recently constructed buildings: notably the House of Hospitality, the Reuben H. Fleet Science Center, the House of Charm, the San Diego Hall of Champions and the Casa de Balboa. Very nice facilities are also available at the Balboa Park Club, located near the International Cottages and the Marie Hitchcock Puppet Theater.

Of special note is the new Blind Community Center at the corner of Upas and Park Boulevard, which offers crafts, exercise, gourmet cooking and computer classes, and a talking books library.

All modern museum exhibits are wheelchair accessible and most have captions for video displays. A call ahead to an individual museum's education office will make it possible for an escorted, narrated tour by a knowledgeable staff member or docent for those with special needs. Several of the institutions offer organized classes and field trip opportunities for children with learning disabilities. With the exception of the historic Marston House, the museums with second stories all now have elevators to upper exhibit areas.

All of the larger museums have special seating available for guests in wheelchairs in their auditoriums and lecture halls. The Old Globe Theatre and the Reuben H. Fleet Science Center also have assistive listening devices available for the hearing-impaired (inquire at the box office). The Space Theater at the Fleet Science Center also offers two IMAX® Dome film screenings daily with captioning.

Gift shops vary with regard to accessibility. Some of the older shops have narrow aisles and higher displays; but you will find the staff members in each of these more than willing to help you find what you're looking for. The same is true of food service. A similar rule of thumb applies–the newer the building, the better the access. Two fast-food places in the Park catering to guests in wheelchairs by providing lower counters, are Galileo's Cafe at the Reuben Fleet and the Time Out Cafe at the Hall of Champions. All of the full-service restaurants have good facilities for the disabled.

As of this writing, wheelchairs (or strollers) are not available for rent in the Park. However there is *a company that will deliver wheelchairs* to the Visitors Center if one is reserved (and paid for with a credit card) in advance: **Mobility Source**, (619) 234-9505.

The Senior Lounge at the Casa del Prado may have a wheelchair you can borrow, but it is offered on a first-come, first-served basis. Call ahead to see if it's available, (619) 236-0262.

> **Hint:** Valet parking is now available in the Plaza de Panama in front of the House of Hospitality every evening and on weekend and holiday afternoons (under $10). Or for a real treat and an easy way to get around in Balboa Park's cultural area, try a pedicab. Pedicabs may not always be on hand in the Park, but you can actually call one to meet you and transport you in the Park as needed. This service is not inexpensive, but is a fun way to go while learning more about the Park from a knowledgeable "driver." Call **Pop's Pedicabs**, (760) 799-4416. Website: **www.popspedicabs.com**

CHAPTER 3
WHERE TO START

First a quick geographical orientation: **Balboa Park is situated on a large mesa intersected by two large canyons**—Cabrillo Canyon on the west and Florida Canyon on the east. **The cultural heart of the Park**—which includes many of the City's museums and theaters, its unique Spanish Colonial architecture, formal gardens, and the famous San Diego Zoo—**is situated on the Central Mesa**.

To the west of Cabrillo Canyon are broad expanses of green lawn—perfect for picnicking—some of the rarest trees and other examples of mature landscaping, the iconic lawn bowling courts, miles of shady green walks, and hiking and bicycling trails. The west side is also the location of the Marston House Museum and Gardens. The West Mesa is bordered by the residential neighborhoods of Hillcrest and Banker's Hill.

Lovely sculpture welcomes visitors to House of Hospitality

To the east of Florida Canyon is an area best known for its outdoor recreational attributes. Here you'll find the Balboa Park  Golf Course (sister course to the famed Torrey Pines links), the Balboa Tennis Club, a velodrome, bocce and petanque courts, a municipal swimming pool and a Frisbee® Golf Course. But you'll also find a native plant demonstration garden, and over four miles of hiking and biking trails in the scrub-filled natural canyon preserve of Florida Canyon itself. The East Mesa area is bordered by the North Park, South Park and Golden Hill residential neighborhoods.

Most people concentrate their visit in the cultural core of the Park on the Central Mesa. This zone is roughly organized in a "T," with major museums situated along El Prado at the top of the "T." Many of these buildings feature Balboa Park's signature Spanish Colonial architecture, which originated with the 1915 Panama-California Exposition. (**For more information on the history of the architecture in the Park, see Chapter 8.**)

This area also includes the Spreckels Organ Pavilion, just south of the Prado, and the Botanical Building slightly to the north. The San Diego Zoo, about a five-minute walk north of El Prado, also had its origins in the 1915 Exposition.

The lower part of the "T" extends south to the Palisades area (Pan American Plaza)—site of much of the activity of the second exposition in 1935-36, and home today of three significant museums, the puppet theater and Starlight Bowl. Both the area along El Prado, and that to the south, in the Palisades area, have been declared national historic landmark areas.

Balboa Park Visitors Center/House of Hospitality

The Balboa Park Visitors Center is located in the first floor northwest corner of the House of Hospitality—right in the heart of the Park. This is an ideal place to begin your exploration. The center, which is staffed by knowledgeable volunteers, is open daily from 9:30 a.m. to 4:30 p.m. The Visitors Center serves close to 500,000 visitors a year.

If you only have three to four hours to spend in the Park, chat with a volunteer for a few minutes to plot out the most rewarding way to spend your time. Let them know if you're more interested in science, art, history, the gardens or the architecture, and what your time and budget constraints might be. They will make suggestions and point you in the right direction.

In addition to providing information for visitors, the historic House of Hospitality offers one of the best restaurants in the city, clean, accessible restrooms, a baby-changing room, an ATM machine, telephones, benches and a cappuccino cart in a sunny courtyard. So well used and loved is the building that it has been called **"The Living Room of San Diego."**

Most parking in this area is no more than a five-minute walk away, and there is a Park tram drop-off adjacent to the House of Hospitality. Fifteen-minute parking is available in the Plaza de Panama, if you want to run in to the Visitors Center to get a quick orientation or directions to the nearest parking lot.

...be sure to pick up the current **"Balboa Park Guide to What's New"**

You'll find an entrance to the Visitors Center under the covered walkway on the north side of the House of Hospitality at the southeast corner of the Plaza de Panama. There's also an entrance off the lovely courtyard in the center of the House of Hospitality.

In addition to free information and advice from the volunteers, be sure to pick up the current **"Balboa Park Guide to What's New"**. This brochure is recommended because it contains current information on all of the exhibitions, musical offerings and theater programs in the Park. It is updated every two months by House of Hospitality staff, and is a complete source of current information on Park events. Exhibits and programs are constantly changing so this tool will be invaluable for your visit. The Visitors Center guide also includes a simple map of the cultural zone of the Park. A small donation for the guide would be much appreciated since the Center is a non-profit operation.

There are many other good maps and books about Balboa Park and San Diego available in the Visitors Center. This is also a good place to pick up brochures on other attractions in the region. **Current bus schedules, free Tuesday info, special event brochures and fliers, Old Town Trolley Tickets, soft drinks, snacks, batteries, aspirin and film are also available.**

There are several free guided tours each week that leave from the Visitors Center—be sure to inquire if one is available on the day of your visit. (More detail on the individual tours available below.)

A new offering at the Visitor Center are audio tours of the cultural zone. For around $5 you rent a hand-held audio device and receive a map showing you the spots where you can dial a number for a colorful description of the museum, garden or other Park feature in front of you. **A children's version is also available.** The narrators inform with a light style and fun details during the estimated 45-minute excursion.

If you wish to delve into Park history and architecture in more detail, you can also purchase **a self-guided walking tour booklet** (two versions available at $3.95 each) by the author of this book, and use it any time of day. Includes a good map of the cultural area with areas of interest highlighted. Each self-guided tour takes about 1 ½ hours.

A few minutes discussing all the options and plotting out your day(s) in Balboa Park can make all the difference...

If you are planning to visit three or more museums while in Balboa Park, you should definitely consider the **Passport to Balboa Park**, also available in the Visitors Center. This is a greatly discounted ticket that admits you to all of the museums that are open during the time of your visit. (Some museums are closed on Mondays, and occasionally museums are closed for renovation or while changing out exhibitions.)

Twelve museums and the Japanese Friendship Garden are included in the Passport, which is accepted for seven days (including the date of purchase) for a one-time visit to each attraction. Again, depending on how many, and which ones you wish to visit, the Passport could save you a considerable amount of money. **The price of the Passport is around $35, but has a value of $95; a children's version sells for about $20. There is also a Zoo/Passport combo available for around $60 for adults and less than $35 for children.**

Talk over your interests with the volunteers. They can show you what the admission prices are for each museum and what the ages for senior and junior pricing are. (Most museums offer a significant discount for these two categories.) If you still can't decide, **ask for a bi-monthly "Guide to What's New," get a cup of coffee and sit down in the courtyard to study it**. A few minutes discussing all the options and plotting out your day(s) in Balboa Park can make all the difference in how much you manage to see and do while visiting the crown jewel of San Diego.

If you haven't already viewed the courtyard with its famous fountain, take time to do so now. This would also be a good time to make a lunch reservation at **The Prado**—the much-praised restaurant just across the courtyard from the Visitors Center. **(For other lunch choices, see Chapter 2.)**

Now you have your Passports and your events guide, a reservation for lunch and hopefully a plan for the day. Ready... begin!

Free tours of the Park

Free guided tours by local experts are offered several days a week. Unless otherwise indicated **these begin and end at the Visitors Center**:

Ranger-led tours

Tours are approximately one hour long. Tour leaders discuss the historical, architectural, and botanical treasures of Balboa Park. **The Park Rangers are committed to helping visitors have a safe and rewarding outdoor experience**. They assist with public safety, raise awareness of conservation needs and methods, and carry out a proactive series of educational activities within the Park and throughout the community. Tour times are subject to change, but are currently at 1 p.m. on Tuesdays and Sundays. Tours begin at the Visitors Center in the House of Hospitality.

Offshoot tours

Offered every Saturday by volunteer horticulturists, the tours meet in front of the Visitors Center at 10:00 a.m., for a one to two hour walk. Tour themes include Balboa Park history (first Saturdays of the month), palm trees (second Saturdays), other trees in the Park (third Saturdays), desert vegetation (fourth Saturdays), and fifth Saturdays an eclectic *"tour del dia."* Inclement weather, or attendance of less than four people, cancels tour. **Offshoot Tours** run from the second Saturday in January through the Saturday before Thanksgiving. Sponsored by the Balboa Park Rangers. Public information: (619) 235-1121.

Architectural tours

Once a month, on the first Wednesday, members of the **Committee of 100 lead tours of the Spanish Colonial architecture** found in the heart of the Park. This group has been raising money since the 1960s to help preserve the beautiful architecture that originated with the 1915 Panama-California Exposition. Tour begins at the Visitors Center at 9:30 a.m., and lasts about one hour.

Natural History Museum Canyoneers

Volunteer naturalists trained in local flora, fauna, and geology, lead guided nature walks in various locations around San Diego County, including Florida Canyon. The walks are offered several times a year. For information call (619) 232-3821 ext. 7, or obtain info via the Web site at www.sdnhm.org

Self-guided tours now available

Of course you may not be able to get to the Park when a free guided tour is being offered. Two recent additions to the services and information available at the Visitors Center give you the means to tour on your own. One must be completed on the day it is started, while the other can be enjoyed either all at one time or in smaller segments over any number of days.

Balboa Park Audio Tours of the historical central core of the Park can be rented at the Visitors Center for around $5 for adults; $4 for juniors and seniors. These involve using a map with numbers which correlate to a keypad on the audio device. Once you access the area you wish to hear about, you simply dial a three-digit code to hear the info. The narrator presents the details in a fun, colorful way, interspersed with the voices of other knowledgeable people, including Architect David Marshall, Author Pam Crooks, Park Ranger Kim Duclo and former Museum Director Arthur Ollman, among others. Complete tour takes about forty-five minutes.

A Walk in Balboa Park # 1 and #2 are self-guided tour booklets which can be purchased for $3.95 each. These pocket-sized guides include detailed information on the history, architecture, and horticulture of the Central and West Mesas of the Park, as well as suggestions on what to see and do while on a visit to Balboa

Park. Sprinkled with anecdotes and charming illustrations, these tours can be taken any time of the day, including early morning or evening when the Park is less crowded and most museums are closed. Each contains detailed walking directions and a map for the area described. Complete tour outlined in each booklet lasts about 1½ hours, but may be broken down into smaller segments and taken over several days.

> **Hint:** The self-guided tour booklets described above would also make a nice gift item to leave behind with a local host/hostess, or to keep on hand for visitors if you live in San Diego.

Other suggested Park walks

If you are already pretty familiar with Balboa Park and would like to explore some new territory, then you might try one of the following, more adventurous walks:

- **Gold Gulch** – Site of a "gold mining camp" during the 1935 California Pacific International Exposition. Besides a simulated mine, "Gold Gulch" had a dance hall, saloon, sheriff's office, shooting gallery, Chinese laundry and a bank with iron-barred windows. Today the ravine west of the Reuben H. Fleet Science Center offers a quiet walk from Zoro Garden, past the San Diego Police Department's horse stable, up a steep hill and out onto President's Way. Access the trail from the south end of Zoro Garden between the Casa de Balboa and the Reuben Fleet Science Center. (*Moderate walk on dirt path and paved street; partial shade; steep climb at the end.*)

- **Palm Canyon** – Take a short walk down a set of wooden steps and along a dirt path to the Balboa Park Club. The canyon covers 2 acres and contains 450 palms of 58 species. The original Mexican fan palms, which are most prominent, date back to the early 1900s. Access the canyon walk from a wooden footbridge, south of the Alcazar Garden parking lot. (*Moderate hike; trail shaded with lush vegetation.*)

- **Old Bridle Trail** – Except for traffic noise from State Highway 163, you could be in the backcountry of San Diego County, amid flowering trees, squirrels and birds. Used primarily by neighborhood residents today, you'll be hiking along an old equestrian trail, now shared with bicyclists. Two easiest places to access the trail—Redwood Circle near lawn bowling courts and picnic area near Seventh Avenue and Upas Street. (*Moderately strenuous conditions, dirt and pavement; 1½ miles in one direction, very steep in places.*)

- **Marston Addition** – Not well known, this portion of the Park was originally attached to the Marston House and Gardens on the Park's west side. Their property straddled Cabrillo Canyon before State Highway 163 bisected it. The Marston family gave this part to the city in the 1940s. On the east side of the highway, you can do a pleasant loop into a residential canyon area where formal trails are being developed. The Marston Addition abuts the Park just west and north of the Boy Scout headquarters on Upas Street.) (*Moderate hiking conditions; partial shade.*)

- **Florida Canyon** – As close to a wilderness hike as you can get in Balboa Park, you'll pass through native vegetation—mostly scrub—and glimpse the animal life that flourishes in this enviroment. Get a feel for what Balboa Park was like before Kate Sessions and others worked their landscaping magic. Three easiest places to access the trail—from the Desert Garden; from the intersection of Pershing Drive, 28th Street, and Florida Drive in Florida Canyon; and southwest of the tennis courts at Morley Field. (*Strenuous walk; 4 ½ miles of dirt paths shared with bicyclists; no shade.*)

- **San Diego Zoo** – Explore over five miles of paved paths in a great setting, enjoying the animals along the way. Make your hike as long or as short as you like, and never see the same thing twice. Best to go early in the day to avoid crowds. Must pay Zoo admission fee or belong as a member. (*Various terrain, steep in places, beautifully landscaped and shady for the most part.*)

Suggested itineraries:
a time-based Balboa Park sampler

With 1-2 hours to spend...your best bet to get a flavor of the Park is to **stroll the Prado area—from Cabrillo Bridge to the Bea Evenson Fountain** (the large fountain at the east end of El Prado)—or **explore the Organ Pavilion** and **Pan American Plaza area. Visit one of the larger museums or two smaller ones, and one garden, or the Botanical Building.**

With 3-4 hours to spend....you could extend your visit north to **Spanish Village** or south towards **Pan American Plaza,** visit **one more museum and one or more of the garden areas.** Take time halfway through to **have a frozen yogurt or cappuccino and people watch.**

When you have the whole day... Start early, **buy a Passport to Balboa Park,** make a reservation for lunch, and **visit a museum or two in the morning with a garden in between.** After lunch **take in a concert,** enjoy a **Park-Ranger-guided or self-guided audio walking tour,** and **visit another museum.** Take time out to relax and people watch! Finish the day with **an IMAX® film at the Fleet Center, a concert at the Organ Pavilion, or a play at the Old Globe.** Opportunities vary depending on the season and day of the week—check at the Visitors Center for current offerings.

Can you combine the Park's cultural core with a trip to the Zoo? This question is frequently asked at the Visitors Center. The answer is yes—if you have a lot of stamina and do some clever planning. Purchase one of the new **"Best of Balboa Park" combo tickets,** which includes a **Passport to Balboa Park** and a **"Best Value" Zoo admission** at the Visitors Center. Since the Center doesn't open until after the Zoo does, try to order your **"Best of Balboa Park" tickets** on-line a few days before (or stop by the Visitors Center the day before you go to pick them up) and start early. **Park behind the House of Charm (where the Mingei International Museum is) in the Alcazar Garden parking lot if possible.**

The Zoo opens earlier than the museums, so enjoy a beautiful walk through the Park during one of the nicest parts of the day and be at the Zoo entrance by 9 a.m. Conserve energy (and your feet!) by purchasing (if you didn't already purchase the combo ticket mentioned above) the "Best Value" ticket package, which includes a guided bus tour, express shuttle bus and an aerial tram ride. The 35-minute narrated bus tour covers a lot of territory and is filled with interesting views and information about this incredible place. After the bus tour you can focus on sections of the Zoo, and forms of wildlife, that most interest you.

Orient yourself with the Zoo's free map. You can even go on-line ahead of time and plan your route (www.sandiegozoo.org/zoo_map.html). Take advantage of moving walkways and escalators whenever possible, and use the aerial tram at least one way across the Zoo to take in the breathtaking views. This will also cut down on long hikes back from the furthest exhibits.

Beat the crowds and **have a leisurely early lunch at Albert's Restaurant** (call ahead, 619-685-3200, or make a reservation when you first arrive), or at one of the many other great spots for lunch. Stop in a gift shop on your way out, and **head back to the El Prado area of the Park by 1 or 1:30**. You still have plenty of time to take in several museums, **visit the Botanical Building**, and even **catch a concert at the Organ Pavilion or folk dancing at the International Cottages** if you visit on a Sunday afternoon. Since you parked near the central plaza in the morning (see how clever that was!) you won't have far to walk to your car at the end of a very rewarding (but tiring) day.

NOTE: *Most museums close by 4:30 or 5 p.m. daily. Some museums stay open later one day a week, generally on Thursday. The Reuben Fleet Science Center stays open until 8 p.m. on Fridays, Saturdays and on Sundays during three-day weekends. All museums host special events from time to time, and may find it necessary to close early. Information regarding special events and hours are generally posted near museum entrances.*

Suggested itineraries: topic-based

It is not easy to categorize museums. Disciplines often overlap. For example, **you might find a traveling exhibit on the science of sports at the Hall of Champions**, or **an art exhibit on quilts at the Museum of San Diego History**. It is strongly suggested that you check with the Balboa Park Visitors Center either by phone (619-239-0512) or on-line (www.balboapark.org) prior to, or when you arrive, for current exhibition and special event information that might be of particular interest to you. But as a quick reference, here is a list organized by general subject matter.

> **Hint:** Check the index for location of more in-depth information on each entry elsewhere in this book.

Interested in art?

- Art Institute
- Balboa Art Conservation Center
- Centro Cultural de la Raza
- Japanese Friendship Garden
- Mingei International Museum
- Museum of Art
- Museum of Photographic Arts (MoPA)
- Photographic Arts building near Spanish Village
- Sculpture Garden at the Museum of Art
- Spanish Village Art Center
- Timken Museum of Art

Interested in science/technology?

- Air and Space Museum
- Automotive Museum
- Earth Fair celebration
- Greater San Diego Science & Engineering Fair
- Mineral and Gem Society
- Model Railroad Museum
- Museum of Man

- Museum of Photographic Arts (MoPA)
- Natural History Museum
- Reuben Fleet Science Center
- San Diego Zoo

Interested in history?

- Air and Space Museum
- Automotive Museum
- Hall of Champions
- House of Hospitality 2nd floor self-guided photo tour
- Marston House
- Model Railroad Museum
- Museum of Man
- Museum of San Diego History
- Park Ranger tours
- Spreckels Organ Pavilion
- Veteran's Museum and Memorial Center

Interested in architecture/landscaping?

- Activity Center and adjacent Garden Court
- Alcazar Gardens
- Bird Park
- Botanical Building
- Botanical Library in Casa del Prado
- Cabrillo Bridge
- California Tower and Building (Museum of Man)
- Casa del Rey Moro Gardens (behind House of Hospitality)
- Committee of 100 Architectural Tours
- El Prado (all of the buildings along the pedestrian promenade)
- House of Hospitality 2nd floor self-guided photo tour
- Japanese Friendship Garden
- Marston House & Gardens

- Offshoot Botanical Tours
- 1935 Cactus Garden
- Palm Canyon
- Pepper Grove playground
- Rose & Cactus Gardens
- San Diego Air & Space Museum (1935 Ford Building)
- San Diego Zoo
- Trees for Health self-guided walk
- Zoro Gardens

Interested in music/performing arts?
- Arican drumming lessons at the World Beat Center
- Ballroom/Swing Dance lessons
- Fern Street Circus
- Jazz/Chamber music concerts at the Museum of Art
- Junior Theatre
- International folk-dancing lessons
- Lawn programs (folk dancing) Sunday afternoons at the International Cottages
- Marie Hitchcock Puppet Theater
- Old Globe Theatre
- Park & Recreation dance classes
- Spreckels Organ concerts
- Starlight Theater
- Street entertainers
- Summer Twilight Concerts
- Ballet Folklorico at the Centro Cultural de la Raza

Interested in sports/recreation?
- Activity Center
- Archery (field & target) ranges
- Athletic fields at Morley Sports Complex
- Badminton at Activity Center
- Balboa Park Golf Course

- Blind Recreation Center
- Bocce/Petanque courts at Morley Field
- Bridge tournaments at Redwood Club
- Bud Kearns Municipal Pool
- Chess at Balboa Club
- Disc (Frisbee®) Golf Course
- Florida Canyon hiking & mountain biking trails
- Hall of Champions Sports Museum
- Horseshoes at Balboa Club
- Kite-flying at Bird Park
- Lawn-bowling courts west of Cabrillo Bridge
- In-line skating on Balboa Drive
- Mountain-biking on the Old Bridle Trail
- Municipal Gym
- Physical Fitness Course at Morley Field Complex
- Quad(riplegic) Rugby
- Table Tennis at Activity Center
- Tennis Courts at Morley Field
- 10K runs in Balboa Park
- Volleyball at Activity Center
- Velodrome
- Wheelchair basketball and tennis tournaments

Evening activities in the Park

More and more activities are being offered in the Park at night as the city grows and audiences expand. Most of the activity is centered on the cultural "T" of the Park along El Prado and President's Way, down to Pan American Plaza. Summer evenings are obviously busier, but there's a surprising amount of nighttime activity most any time of year.

There is something magical about walking down the Prado in the early evening with little lights twinkling in the trees and the sound of water playing in the fountains. General lighting of the walkways and parking lots has been improved in the last few years. Accent lighting now showcases some of the major architectural features in the Park, creating a lovely atmosphere at night.

In the summer, dozens of San Diegans **picnic in Balboa Park** prior to one of the **Twilight Concerts at the Organ Pavilion**, or before an **evening performance at Starlight Bowl or the Old Globe Theatre**. Both Starlight Bowl and the Old Globe's Festival Stage offer professional productions under the stars in warmer months. Also in the summer, you might find jazz on the steps at the Museum of Art or a silent film at the Organ Pavilion accompanied by the mighty Spreckels instrument. Even **the San Diego Zoo** has begun offering excursions into the **"Nighttime Zoo" in the summer**.

Almost year-round you can attend evening **plays and musicals at the Casa del Prado Theater** or the **Old Globe's two indoor venues**. Most museums offer **lectures and classes after hours** on a regular basis, and some, like the Museum of Art and Museum of Photographic Arts (MoPA), are regularly open one evening a week, generally on Thursdays. The Reuben Fleet Science Center is open until 8 p.m. or later on weekends and holidays; other days they close at 5 p.m. (For current museum hours and special evening activities, check **www.balboapark.org,** click on "Calendar" and then the "After Dark" button. You can also link to every museum's Web site from the main site.

With so many cultural institutions gathered in one place, there may be dozens of special interest group meetings, lectures, film screenings, music and dance lessons and rehearsals, and theater performances on any one night in the Park. Most of these activities are geared towards members and volunteers, but some are open to the public. Inquire at the Visitors Center to find out about upcoming public events of interest.

Many of the institutions (including the San Diego Zoo) have space available for rent for catered functions, and are well-used in the evenings for this purpose. **Business and social functions of all sizes take place throughout the Park**, with the hub of this activity centered at the House of Hospitality. **The Prado restaurant** located there is **one of the most popular spots in the city for special event dining**.

For individuals or smaller groups, the dining room is normally open until 9 p.m., Tuesday through Thursday, 10 p.m. on Friday and Saturday, and 8 p.m. on Sunday. The bar remains open one hour after the dining room closes. Outdoor seating is available on the terraces during warmer months. This place really hums with activity on weekends. Advance reservations are recommended-especially for pre-show dining. Phone: (619) 557-9441.

To inquire about hosting a private event for 30 – 1,500 people at the House of Hospitality, call (619) 232-9333. For information about other facility rentals available, call the institution you're interested in directly, or the manager of the Balboa Park Visitors Center, (619) 231-9494.

The San Diego Park and Recreation Department also rents space for special events and activities within the Park. Check at the Administration Building (at Inspiration Point Way and Park Boulevard) for information on holding events in indoor public facilities (call 619-235-1103) or in various outdoor locations around the Park (619-235-1169). Certain restrictions apply. **For groups larger than 75 you must have a permit for outdoor gatherings.** Call (619) 235-1104 for more information.

Sunday afternoons in the Park

Every day is special in Balboa Park, but **if you have only one day and you can arrange it, make it a Sunday**. Trams run more frequently, Park Rangers give tours, and all the museums are open—many with special programs or demonstrations. **More outdoor entertainment is available, most art fairs, festivals and flower shows take place on a Sunday**. With more folks around, the atmosphere is just generally more festive. People-watching is superb.

On the downside, traffic is worse and parking at a premium. Sundays are one of the biggest days for Zoo attendance; the Zoo traffic and parking can affect other park users. Traffic on Park Blvd., with cars searching for parking close to the cultural institutions, can cause gridlock. But with a little advance planning, even a visit on a Sunday in August, can be one of the most memorable experiences you'll ever have in Balboa Park.

Balboa Park is one of the most popular locations in the city for 5K and 10K runs/walks (averaging two events per month). These events often take place on Sunday morning. Usually they start very early, around 7:30 a.m., but this offers a great way to get into the Park and obtain parking on the busiest day of the week.

In any case, **try to arrive by 9 a.m.**, when plenty of parking is still available. Grab a coffee and a muffin, a **"Guide to What's New"** at the Visitors Center, and sit in the courtyard at the House of Hospitality to plan your day. While there, if you haven't done so already, **make a reservation for an early lunch at The Prado**, or one of the other restaurants in or near the Park recommended in Chapter 2.

Visit a museum or two, take a garden walk or **hike in Florida Canyon**. Alternately, you could take one of the Park trams for a quick orientation to the Park, get off on the West side of Cabrillo Bridge and walk back along El Prado to the House of Hospitality. Now you've built up an appetite for a hearty lunch that will hold you well through the afternoon's activities!

After your meal, take a **Park Ranger-led tour at 1 p.m.** from the Visitors Center to learn more about the history and the architecture of the buildings. Or stroll through the **Botanical Building** enjoying the seasonal display of flowering plants.

But be back at the **Spreckels Organ Pavilion** by 2 for the free pipe organ concert that's given every week—rain or shine. This is the world's largest outdoor pipe organ, built for the 1915 Panama-California Exposition, so you'll be able to hear the opening notes from almost any location in the cultural center of the Park. But, for the best sound, try to get a good seat in the center section.

If you prefer, wander over to the **International Cottages for folk dancing** on the outdoor stage, also at 2 p.m. The cottages are open on Sundays from 12 to 4 p.m. (February through mid- November only). If you'd like to try your skills at folk dancing, free demonstrations (feel free to join in) are available at the nearby Balboa Park Club on Sunday afternoons from 12:30 to 5 p.m.

> Visit a museum or two, take a garden walk or hike in Florida Canyon.

Sample some of the goodies prepared by the volunteer hosts in the open houses. And while in the vicinity, don't miss the **U.N. Association International Gift Shop** featuring handcrafted gifts, books, UNICEF cards, music CDs, and confections from around the world.

Spend the rest of the afternoon taking in another museum or two, an outdoor art show or an indoor flower show (check the

"What's New" guide you picked up earlier at the Visitor Center for a current schedule of special events).

Browse in the various studios of **Spanish Village Art Center.** Stop along El Prado and enjoy the **street entertainers** that usually perform there on Sundays. The quality of the entertainment goes up on weekends when there's a larger audience.

If you have young children, several not-to-be missed options are open to you on Sundays. **"Ms. Frizzle**™**"** of Scholastic Publishing's *The Magic School Bus*© fame appears **at the Natural History Museum** with two free shows on Sundays only. (Call 619-232-3821 ext. 8 for times.) Three puppet shows are performed on Sunday, while **the Carousel** and **Miniature Train Ride** remain open all afternoon. Plan a picnic at **Pepper Grove** or by "The Big Fig" tree behind Natural History. You could also visit the Museum of Man's **"Children's Discovery Center"** or the Reuben Fleet Science Center's **"Kid City"**

> **Hint:** Although St. Paul's Cathedral is not technically in Balboa Park, a beautiful event takes place at 5 p.m. every Sunday across Sixth Avenue on the corner of Nutmeg and Sixth (on the west side). An Anglican Evensong service is offered in a musical and liturgical style dating back to the 17th century. Cathedral choirs, including one of only five boys' choirs in the United States to sing this style of music, perform. For more information, call: (619) 298-7261.

Summer vs. winter

San Diego enjoys good sightseeing weather year-round, but the addition of several hours of daylight in the late spring and summer months affords some additional opportunities for fun in Balboa Park. The Zoo stays open late during a **"Nighttime Zoo" promotion between mid-June and Labor Day**. Many of the museums target the peak tourist season to bring in special traveling exhibitions and extend their hours. A few stay open later on Thursday evenings. Some, like the Museum of Art, offer jazz concerts or other musical events on a regular basis. The Puppet Theater, Carousel and Miniature Train offer added programs and hours of operation during summer months. There are fewer school groups in the Park on field trips, but many day camps schedule trips to the Park in the summer.

Free musical concerts of all kinds are given at the Organ Pavilion four evenings a week. The Old Globe's outdoor **Festival Stage and Starlight Bowl offer regular performances**. A drive through the Park early on a summer evening will reveal that the art of picnicking is alive and well in San Diego. Many an elegant picnic is spread on shady lawns in the Park preceding a nighttime musical or Shakespearean performance.

There is no better time for a picnic, wedding or family gathering in Balboa Park than summertime. The weather is almost always glorious from Memorial Day through Labor Day, with one exception—"June Gloom."

Due to a San Diego phenomenon created by coastal weather patterns in May and June, **skies are often overcast in the morning with a deep marine layer of clouds**; it usually clears up in the early afternoon, but the evenings are cool and slightly damp for the same reason. Just **bring along sweaters and blankets for outdoor activities**, especially in the evening.

The months of **August and September usually bring the hottest weather, but** Balboa Park's location close to the bay and ocean moderates the temperatures a bit. Fortunately we don't experience the high humidity levels of other parts of the country in the summer; our heat tends to be very dry. If planning a hike or other strenuous outdoor activity in the Park, be sure to pack plenty of water and sunscreen.

If you're a casual day visitor and can't take the heat, **stick to the covered walkways, cool museum interiors and garden areas**. Or park yourself near one of the Park's many fountains in a shady spot and have a frozen lemonade—you'll be ready to explore more of the Park's wonders in no time!

Naturally parking is impacted by higher usage in the summer months. As a result the free tram service extends its hours and adds an extra tram on the route, thereby reducing the wait time. Check the summer tram schedule in the Visitors Center, or at each tram stop, for the last pick-up of the day.

A rainy day in Balboa Park—a special treat

San Diego is known for its beaches and beautiful climate, but contrary to the image commonly portrayed by the visitor industry it does have weather. Maybe not of the Minnesota variety, but **we do get rain and cool temperatures occasionally.** Yup, even down in the forties on rare occasion. While to a Canadian here in February, this may seem like spring, to visitors who brought their shorts and T-shirts for rollerskating by the bay, the dip in temperature may put a damper on the vacation.

What better time to explore some of the finest museums in the country than a day like this? Come early, buy a Passport to Balboa Park, make a reservation for lunch or pack a picnic to enjoy under a covered walkway, and peruse a current map/guide from the Visitor Center to find the exhibits/programs that interest you the most.

Use the free Park tram to get from the Prado down to the Palisades area. Don't worry if you didn't bring an umbrella— you can usually dash from museum to museum without getting too wet!

If the weather clears up later, go over to the Zoo, or on one of the recommended garden walks. There will be no crowds and everything will be beautifully green and fresh. **Guaranteed to be one of the nicest days you'll ever spend in this fair city.**

CHAPTER 4
HOW TO VISIT THE PARK ON A BUDGET

Obviously it's possible to visit Balboa Park without spending any money since it is a public space. Many San Diegans visit on a daily basis walking their dog, bicycling or jogging along its many paths. One can bring a picnic, take a free walking tour of the gardens and architectural features, or enjoy a musical concert at the Organ Pavilion without ever spending a dime. But a trip to Balboa Park without taking in at least a few of its paid cultural attractions is to miss out on a key component of its specialness.

Botanical Building is "a must"— and it's free

First some background info. There are more than 85 cultural institutions with offices or programs in Balboa Park. Most of the City's museums are located here as well as several major theater and dance groups—and of course the world-famous San Diego Zoo. By city charter, these organizations must be non-profit to carry on their activities in the Park. The city owns all of the buildings and oversees agreements with the organizations to manage the facilities. Other than having the buildings provided (which of course is not insignificant), and receiving funding from hotel and motel taxes, which represents only a small part of their budget, the organizations must pay their own way. Gone are the days of major subsidies from government for museums and other cultural institutions in San Diego.

Therefore, as in most cities in the United States, it is necessary for the institutions to charge admission to support their operation. **Admission prices in Balboa Park vary from museum to museum.** Some of the smaller institutions charge only $5 or $6, while the larger ones charge as much as $9-12 for regular adult admission.

Passport to Balboa Park/ 'Best of Balboa Park' combo tickets

In 1986, the museums that charge admission created the **Passport to Balboa Park**, making it easier and less expensive to visit several museums on one visit to the Park. Pay one price and a one-time visit to nearly all of the museums is included. (**Usually the Passport admission includes a museum's permanent collection; there may be an additional charge to see a traveling exhibit**).

PASSPORT TO BALBOA PARK

A Passport is valid for one week from date of purchase. If you can't extend your visit to the Park, purchasing a Passport may still make financial sense. A visit to four of the largest museums can total several dollars more than the cost of a Passport. So even if you don't get to all of the museums, you'll still save money. Even better, there is now **a Passport/Zoo combo called "Best of Balboa Park,"** which can also be used over the course of seven days. It **includes the "Best Value" admission package at the Zoo and admission to almost all the museums in the heart of the Park for around $60 for adults; $33 for kids.**

Check regular admission prices and the current price of a Passport in the Visitors Center where volunteers and staff are also available to answer questions. At this writing, admission to 13 cultural attractions is included in an adult Passport for only $35; if you were to pay full price for admission to each of these it would cost over $95!! Children's Passports are available for around $20.

The Passport is intended as a discount on regular adult admission prices to the museums; it may not represent a savings on senior admission since these are usually significantly discounted rates. Purchase Passports to Balboa Park at the Visitors Center, or at any one of the participating museums. If you have a group of 10 or more, it's possible to arrange purchase of the Passports in advance through the Passport to Balboa Park office. Call (619) 231-1640.

NOTE: *The Passport program is undergoing changes that will make it even easier to use. Soon you may receive a "credit card" that can be swiped at each museum you wish to visit. Also, be aware that as admission prices change every year or so, the price of a Passport will go up accordingly.*

Free Tuesdays

If you happen to visit on one of the **first four Tuesdays of the month**, take advantage of another program designed to make Balboa Park's attractions more affordable. As part of the museums' financial arrangements with the City of San Diego, they open their doors to the public, free of charge, one day a month. **Many museums now restrict Free Tuesday to San Diego County residents and active-duty military only.** Check at the Visitor Center for current policy. A pretty consistent schedule has evolved over the years, taking place on the same day each month. These have come to be known as **Free Tuesdays**.

Visit on the first Tuesday of the month, for example, and you can take in the exhibit galleries at the Reuben Fleet Science Center and the San Diego Natural History Museum, then see the scale model trains running at the San Diego Model Railroad Museum; on the second Tuesday, the Veteran's Museum and Memorial Center, Museum of San Diego History, and Museum of Photographic Arts (MoPA) open their doors, and so on. See Chapter 10, page 159 For a complete listing. Be sure to check on-line at **www.balboapark. org** or at the Visitors Center for a current schedule.

As you might imagine, the **exhibit galleries get pretty crowded on Free Tuesdays**, especially during the summer months and holiday periods. Plan accordingly and come early. **During the school year, your best bet is to come later in the day when school groups have left the Park** to return to the classroom—say, after 1 p.m.

Founder's Day at the Zoo

The San Diego Zoo does not participate in the Free Tuesdays program but does open its gates to the public one day a year on **Founder's Day**—the first Monday in October. Needless to say, thousands of people turn out for this event, creating traffic jams on the main thoroughfares and on Zoo walkways. But it's a wonderful opportunity to visit one of the world's greatest Zoos at no charge. Come early, take public transportation, and bring a picnic lunch— the whole day will be much more enjoyable. Also, during the last few years children (11 and under) have been admitted free of charge for the entire month of October.

Museum Month

February is **Museum Month in San Diego**, offering another chance to see not only museums in Balboa Park but throughout the city at low cost. This involves picking up a "culture card" at one of the big department stores in town (check with the Visitors Center or any of the museums to find out which store is participating this year) to received a hefty discount at each museum you visit. The program is organized by the **San Diego Museum Council** (619-276-0101). Understandably certain restrictions apply. Museum Month is a great program designed to give you a taste of the cultural offerings available in this city.

Balboa Park December Nights

Another opportunity to visit the museums of Balboa Park free of charge is on the first Friday and Saturday in December every year, during **December Nights**. Balboa Park's holiday "gift to San Diego," features not only **free admission to museums from 5 to 9 p.m.**, but **special entertainment, craft booths and food offerings throughout the Park from 5 to 10 p.m. on Friday and noon to 10 p.m. on Saturday**. Organized in 1978 by the cultural institutions, the event has grown to one of the largest outdoor festivals in Southern California. Balboa Park December Nights typically draws as many as 100,000 people each day, but retains a charming, homespun holiday atmosphere despite the crowds. **Free parking is available at the San Diego Zoo** (though not usually open for December Nights), **along Park Boulevard and Sixth Avenue, and at the Inspiration Point parking lots**. Vehicular traffic is banned from the interior of the Park; however **free shuttles transport visitors** to convenient drop-off points. Plan for large crowds and traffic delays (or take public transportation), dress warmly, and have a plan of action.

Go on-line (**www.balboapark.org**) and **print a schedule of December Nights activities**, along with a good map of the museums and entertainment areas, and study it before heading out into the Park. The schedule is usually available a few days before the event. If you don't have access to the Web, **stop by the Visitors Center first, before doing anything else**. There are other information booths, but often the volunteers aren't as familiar with the park as the Visitor Center staff and volunteers are.

At the same time, **pick up the latest edition of the "What's New in Balboa Park"** (donation suggested) to learn what exhibits and programs are currently available in the museums. There is no way you can get around to all the museums in one night and really enjoy the experience. If you have done your homework first, you'll know which museums not to miss, what food booths are a must, and which musical entertainment the family will enjoy most.

NOTE: *Passports to Balboa Park, Free Tuesdays and Balboa Park December Nights museum admissions **may not include special traveling exhibitions, films or programs**. The museums' regular exhibit galleries featuring their permanent collections are almost always available for these types of admissions. Occasionally a museum or gallery will be closed for installation of a new exhibition or remodeling.*

Also check out the Balboa Park page in the *San Diego Union-Tribune* each week in **Thursday's "Night & Day" section**, and the **calendar of events section of *The Reader*,** (free weekly publication that comes out on Thursday) to find out about freebies in the Park.

Always free

Always free, and almost always available during a day visit to Balboa Park, are the **Timken Museum** (closed only on Mondays and the entire month of September) and the **Botanical Building** (closed on Thursdays and public holidays). Combine a visit to one or both of these, with an inexpensive self-guided walking or free Park Ranger-led tour (on Tuesdays and Sundays), or a Park and Recreation Department-sponsored historical or botanical tour on Saturdays. **Take a free tram ride to the west side of the Park**, bordered by Sixth Avenue, and walk back across the Cabrillo Bridge. You'll see British-style lawn bowling almost every afternoon between 1 and 3 p.m.

> Almost every weekend you can also take in a free flower show...

On any Sunday afternoon, spread a picnic, purchase a soft-serve ice cream or yogurt for dessert, and **browse through the artists' studios in Spanish Village Art Center**. Afterwards stroll down El Prado, and south along Pan American Road, to the **Spreckels Organ Pavilion for a free organ concert** at 2 p.m., or visit the House of Pacific Relations' International Cottages for ethnic treats and folk-dancing from around the world.

Almost every weekend you can also take in a free flower show, see some pretty good street entertainers, and try your hand at African drumming at the World Beat Center. Gardens and playgrounds are always open and free (with the exception of the Japanese Friendship Garden, which charges a very low admission).

Inexpensive for children

Just across Park Blvd., by way of a footbridge, is the Rose Garden, where a **collection of miniature roses** will delight little ones. Back on the west side of Park Blvd., and one block north is the Carousel and the ride-on Miniature Train, which only cost $1.25 each. Children under 15 are always free (with an adult) at the Model Railroad Museum in the Casa de Balboa and at the Art Institute in the House of Charm. In the Palisades area, **inexpensive puppet shows are performed twice daily** Wednesday through Friday mornings, with added shows on weekends, holidays, and during the summer months.

Take older children on a nature hike in Florida Canyon (access the trail from the Desert Garden on the east side of Park Boulevard, just north of the Rose Garden, or near the tennis courts at Morley Field); play Disc Golf (around $2.50) at Morley Field; or fly kites in Bird Park. Table tennis and volleyball courts are available for open play at various times during the week at the Activity Center on Park Boulevard, and **in-line skating and bike-riding are popular activities along the Sixth Avenue side of the Park.** Mountain biking is also allowed on various hiking trails throughout the Park. **(See Chapter 9 for other ideas for kids.)**

Other ways to save money

There are two other ways to save money on a visit to Balboa Park, especially **if you live in, or frequently visit the San Diego area.** Join one or more of the Park's organizations, and you'll generally receive free admission to that museum's exhibit galleries, as well as invitations to special events throughout the year.

One real bargain is a membership in the San Diego Zoological Society, which includes unlimited admission for the member and several guest passes that can be used at either the Zoo or the San Diego Wild Animal Park (located in north San Diego County, near Escondido). **Ideally, you should join the Zoo, and at least one or two other organizations in the Park** - that interest you. Not just for the freebies of course, but because your support as a member helps ensure the future success of these organizations.

Take that interest one step further—as a Park volunteer—and you will be doubly rewarded. No matter what your interest, you'll undoubtedly find something to match it. If concern for the environment is important to you, volunteer for Earth Day activities and join the San Diego Natural History Museum. Love photography? **Offer your time and talents at MoPA, or another art museum of your choice.** They all need volunteers—to help with everything from cataloguing work in the archives, to serving as museum docents, to fund-raising.

Restoring old airplanes or automobiles your thing? **The San Diego Air and Space** or **Automotive Museums** are looking for you. **Volunteer opportunities abound in the Park for puppetry, dance, astronomy or local history enthusiasts as well as for**

people interested in theater, gardening or sports. The list goes on and on. All of these organizations offer lectures, receptions and special performances with guest artists and experts in their field, to which volunteers are invited.

Check the *San Diego Union-Tribune's* "Currents" section on the first Friday of every month for a complete listing of volunteer opportunities in San Diego-many of them in Balboa Park. Or **call the United Way, Retired Senior Volunteer Program, the Balboa Park Visitors Center or any of the institutions** you're interested in, to find out about volunteer opportunities.

What to See and Do

CHAPTER 5
CULTURAL ATTRACTIONS

Many great cities have urban parks with beautifully landscaped spaces where people can escape the congestion and pressures of life in a metropolis. And a few have one or two museums, a Zoo or a planetarium within their boundaries. But only in San Diego can you find many of the city's largest cultural institutions, including museums, theaters and a zoological park in the heart of its largest park. Only five minutes from downtown and 10 minutes from the airport!

New and old blend in Balboa Park

Geographically, most of the attractions are located in the cultural "T" zone formed by El Prado and Pan American Plaza. All except for the Marston House are located in the Central Mesa area. See map for exact locations.

For a thematic listing of cultural opportunities - art, history, science, etc., check the suggested topic-based itineraries in Chapter 3, on starting on page 63.

Cultural attractions are listed alphabetically by the full name of the institution and organized under two headings: 1. Museums and Other Attractions and 2. Performing (Lively) Arts.

NOTE: *Many organization names are preceded by "San Diego," and therefore will be listed under "S." If you have trouble finding the one you're looking for, check the subject index under the most commonly used name.*

MUSEUMS AND OTHER ATTRACTIONS
with contributions by Mary Anderson and Roger Conlee

Centro Cultural de La Raza

A huge water tank, built during the Second World War as an auxiliary water supply for the Navy Hospital, has become a unique center dedicated to creating, promoting, and preserving Chicano, Mexican, and Native American art and culture. It began when a group calling themselves the Artistas del Barrio persuaded the Park and Recreation Department to allow them the use of the Ford Building.

In 1970, other uses were planned for that building, and the group was offered the water tank in the Pepper Grove area. They moved in, and the building was dedicated July 11, 1971.

The Centro Cultural de La Raza is well known for its decorative, colorful murals around the outside of the building, located on Park Boulevard. Several of the artists who painted the significant murals in San Diego's Chicano Park helped decorate the exterior of the Centro.

Inside, there is an art gallery, which has rotating exhibits, a small gift and book shop, and a performance space where theater, dance, music, and film/video programs are presented year-round.

Ongoing programs include Sunday Zapateado, presented by Target on the second Sunday each month and the third Sunday of the month, Centro Mercado from noon to 4 p.m., where visual artists exhibit and sell their unique creations. In addition, Ballet Folklorico en Aztlan presents a different region of Mexico each month and is free to the public.

Tours and workshops are available when arranged in advance. The gallery and gift shop are open Tuesday-Sunday, 12 to 4 p.m. Admission: free (donation suggested). For public information check their website **www.centroraza.com**, or call (619) 235-6135.

George White and Anna Gunn
Marston House Museum & Gardens

Set apart from the other museums in the northwest corner of the Park is an historic gem: **The Marston House and Gardens**. Constructed in 1905 for successful merchant, civic leader and **Balboa Park activist George W. Marston**, and his wife Anna, the home harkens back to life in San Diego prior to the two expositions in the Park.

The design is representative of an emerging architectural style at the time, known as the American Arts and Crafts Movement. Shunning the elaborate, ornate features common to Victorian homes of the late 19th century, San Diego architects **William Hebbard and Irving Gill** chose instead to focus on function and simplicity of design.

Beautiful woodwork, including many built-ins, ample windows framing views of the surrounding five acres of landscaped grounds, and a feeling of spaciousness characterize a style reminiscent of **Frank Lloyd Wright, whom Gill worked with in Chicago in the late 1800s**.

Among other notable achievements of George Marston's life, was the founding of the **San Diego Historical Society**. The Marston home was generously bequeathed to the city, and the grounds annexed to Balboa Park by the Marston family in 1974. The San Diego Historical Society maintains and operates the museum. The home has been authentically restored and decorated with furniture and art representative of the early 1900s. Today the **Marston House is listed on the National Register of Historic Places**, and is well worth a visit.

The grounds are also worthy of exploration. Kate Sessions, along with several nationally known landscape architects, was a consultant on the original landscaping. Many of the trees and plants she chose have reached full maturity. Hal Walker and William Templeton Johnson (architect of the San Diego Museum of Art and the San Diego Natural History Museum) designed the formal garden to the north of the house in an English Romantic style to commemorate the Marstons' 50th wedding anniversary in 1927. Today it's a popular Balboa Park wedding site.

The garden and grounds are open daily, free of charge. The home may be viewed for a modest fee on **weekends only—Friday, Saturday and Sunday from 10 a.m. to 4:45 p.m. Guided tours leave at 10 and 11 a.m., 1, 2, 3 and 4 p.m.** During the 45-minute docent-guided tour you'll hear more about the Marston family, the home's architecture and anecdotes on life in the early 20th century. Last tour leaves promptly at 4 p.m.

The Marston House and Gardens are located at 3525 Seventh Avenue, on the corner of Upas Street and Seventh Avenue. The free Park tram's nearest drop-off is at Quince Street and Sixth Avenue, a few blocks away. It's a pleasant walk from there. For more information, call (619) 298-3142, (619) 232-6203, or visit the San Diego Historical Society's extensive Web site: **www.sandiegohistory.org**. Call for outdoor wedding info. (619) 235-1169.

House of Pacific Relations/Hall of Nations

A group of small international cottages was built for the 1935 Exposition, to represent the houses of the masses, the common people, during the colonial period in Mexico. Representatives of countries exhibiting at the fair, mainly those of Latin American democracies, used the little houses for national headquarters.

Each cottage was furnished by the country represented and hosted throughout the fair by natives in costumes appropriate to its folkways. The cottages proved so popular that when the fair closed, the groups formed a permanent organization, which they named the "House of Pacific Relations."

The purpose of the organization is to foster and cultivate a spirit of understanding, tolerance and good will, and to present to the public the traditions, music and culture of each represented nation.

During the Second World War the cottages were used by the Navy, but in 1948 were returned to their former occupants. In 1962, the House of Pacific Relations was incorporated as a non-profit organization.

The cottages are open to the public **Sunday afternoons from noon to 4 p.m.** Cottage "natives" dress in traditional costumes and display the arts and culture of their homelands. Ethnic foods are also available. From February through mid-November, outdoor programs of folk dancing and music are presented at 2 p.m.

Thirty-one nations are represented, including Argentina, Austria, China, Colombia, Czech and Slovak Republics, Denmark, England, Finland, France, Germany, Hungary, Iran, Ireland, Israel, Italy, Lithuania, Norway, Palestine, Panama, Philippines, Poland, Puerto Rico, Scotland, Spain, Sweden, Turkey, Ukraine, and the United States of America.

The Hall of Nations nearby serves as the headquarters for the House of Pacific Relations. During the 1915 Exposition, the Hall of Nations facility was known as the "Utah" building. For the second expo it was used as a press club; during the Second World War it served as officers' quarters; and for many years between the expos and after (1923-71), was home to the San Diego Floral Association. Now, it's used for displays by members of the House of Pacific Relations, and is also occupied by the House of Italy. Public information: (619) 234-0739. Web site: **www.sdhpr.org**.

Mingei International Museum

The Mingei International Museum, a treasure house of folk art, can be found in the **House of Charm on the Park's main Plaza de Panama.**

At any one time, three to six exhibitions present colorful handmade objects from diverse cultures. **The Mingei is dedicated to furthering and displaying the art of all the world's peoples**.

Upon entering, you'll see a large display gallery to the left and a lofty rotunda directly ahead, in which may be hanging giant masks, an oversized balloon splashed with the colors of the rainbow, or some other huge feast for the senses. If nothing hangs there, look to the large wall to the right, which might display an extravagant tapestry or handmade native costume.

When you've had your fill of the exhibits on the ground level, take the stairs to the second floor, where more sensory delights await.

Some traveling exhibits are shown, but 95 percent of the displays are assembled from the Mingei's permanent collection, which comprise more than 10,000 pieces.

The museum's name gives some visitors the misconception that the Mingei is a Japanese museum. **The word "Mingei" was coined by the Japanese scholar Soetsu Yanagi. In Japanese, "Min" means "all people" and "gei" is "art,"** and this museum truly represents art from all cultures, not just Asian.

Dr. Yanagi recognized that the things people use-pots, vases, toys, beds, chairs, coats, wardrobes-can be art. Yet, unlike paintings and sculpture, they are often discarded when people are through with them. Believing that examples of these human creations should be preserved, Yanagi founded the Mingei Association, which celebrates "the wholeness of man's spirit."

Launched modestly as a toy show in 1974, by former San Diego State University art instructor Martha Longenecker, the new museum in San Diego flourished and moved into the rebuilt House of Charm when it reopened in Balboa Park in 1996.

To the right of the entrance is the elegant **Collectors' Gallery**. As the name implies, it's more than a gift shop. Available are coffee table art books, and one-of-a-kind original items, including **bowls, dolls, hand-lacquered birds and animals, and pieces related to specific exhibitions. Wearable art includes coats, dresses, silk shawls, vests and saris.** No tee-shirts and ball caps here.

Allow at least an hour for Mingei International, which is open from 10 a.m. to 4 p.m. Tuesday through Sunday. For more information, call (619) 293-0003. The Web address is: **www.mingei.org**.

NOTE: *Mingei International Museum also operates a North County satellite facility in Escondido. For more information call the Balboa Park museum or check out their Web site.*

Museum of Photographic Arts

Who doesn't like looking at pictures? Sight may be the most satisfying of the senses and the **Museum of Photographic Arts**

(MoPA) always provides a visual feast. The museum quadrupled its exhibit space with a major renovation and expansion in 1999.

The museum carries out its mission of collecting and exhibiting the entire spectrum of the photographic medium in dramatic style, offering park visitors thought-provoking displays from great photographers of past and present. Exhibits developed from the museum's permanent collection are shown on a rotating basis, as are significant traveling exhibits.

MoPA's expansion offers 28,000 feet of exhibition space, a library, a 226-seat theater/lecture hall, a large reception lobby, a dedicated classroom, and a room for viewing photographic prints. MoPA also has a new, 5,000-square-foot workshop for preparing exhibits, and a chilled, humidity-controlled storage vault.

...offering Park visitors thought-provoking displays from great photographers of past and present.

Having grown in stature and reputation since its inception in 1983, MoPA now creates its own exhibitions for travel. For example, a MoPA-developed exhibit, "The Model Wife," toured art museums in Paris, Chicago and Cleveland. Another, "Abellardo Morell and the Camera Eye," has toured major Eastern and Midwestern cities.

The permanent collection traces the history of photography, from Daguerreotypes and salt prints to digital photography. The holdings run to more than 9,000 photographs and **include works by Matthew Brady, Edward Steichen, Margaret Bourke-White, Ansel Adams and other U.S. camera greats.** The museum also has a large collection from Latin American photographic artists. Museums and university galleries may borrow displays from the collection.

Learning through photography is a key part of MOPA's mission. Its Education Advisory Committee, made up of teachers, scholars and art educators, helped to develop the Visual Classroom, designed for grades four through twelve. Funded by the National Endowment for the Arts, the program includes teacher workshops and student field trips to teach visual literacy and critical thinking skills through photography.

The photographic library holds over 20,000 volumes and is now open to museum members and advanced researchers. There is a separate print viewing room in the museum where educators and researchers may view photographs from the permanent collection. The library and print viewing rooms are available by appointment only.

The atrium area may be rented by organizations and groups for private affairs and functions. A variety of film- and photography-related books and gifts are offered for sale at the museum store. Ph: (619) 238-7559. Web site: **www.MoPA.org**.

Museum of San Diego History and Research Library

In the Museum of San Diego History's 8,800 square feet of exhibit space, you'll see **ever-changing exhibits from the San Diego Historical Society's collection,** as well as traveling displays. Countless artifacts, catalogued and stored in the museum basement, are brought out on a rotating basis to form these interesting exhibitions.

The emphasis is on the colorful history of the San Diego region, but not exclusively so. You might see a lavish display of costumes and sets used over the years by the San Diego Opera, or an exhibition on "the marketing of Southern California," fascinating tourism ads, posters and brochures from the past.

Maybe you'll spot great-grandma's sun bonnet among the museum's costume collection, which includes old dresses, suits, hats, shoes and other clothing accessories from bygone days.

Historical lectures are presented in the Hans and Margaret Doe Education Center. The 100-seat Thornton Theater is the site of film showings and other educational programs.

The museum's Education Department conducts educational and outreach programs. Along with other park institutions and the Price-Weingart Foundation, the museum has **established a special educational partnership with San Diego's Rosa Parks Elementary School.**

You'll find the Historical Society's Research Library on the level below the main exhibit area. **The archives house one of the nation's largest photo collections, with 2.5 million images.** Photographs, slides, postcards, and film and glass-plate negatives, the latter kept in a chilled room, comprise the vast collection, which includes decades worth of photos from *The San Diego Union-Tribune* and the Ticor Title Insurance Company.

The Archives house one of the nation's largest photo collections, with 2.5 million images.

Reproductions of historic photos may be purchased, with certain limitations on their use.

The Research Archives also include manuscripts, newspapers, architectural drawings, maps and oral histories. Historical Society members may use the archives at no cost; others must pay a modest fee. (Society memberships start at $50.)

Books on local history, prints of historic photos and locally made gifts are featured in the **charming museum gift shop.**

The museum also operates the **George and Anna Gunn Marston House and Gardens** in the northwest corner of Balboa Park, as well as the **Villa Montezuma** and **Serra Museum**-two historic and interesting sites outside the Park. (Admission to the Museum of San Diego History does *not* provide admission to the other sites.) Detailed information on the Marston House may be found elsewhere in this chapter. Phone: (619) 232-6203; or visit the society's extensive Web site: **www.sandiegohistory.org**.

Reuben H. Fleet Science Center

Stop by the Fleet Science Center on a busy afternoon and you'll find out why this museum is so popular. It's a colorful, joyful place where kids and adults can relax, make discoveries together, and learn something about the rapidly changing world of science and technology.

Entering the building from the Prado side, you'll find an attractive two-story rotunda with a large high-tech ticket and information counter. Opening off the entry rotunda are **Galileo's Café** and the **North Star Science store**. This can be a congested area on busy days, but the staff is very helpful and lines move quickly.

Major renovations and an expansion to the Fleet Center nearly doubled its size to more than 93,000 square feet. There is **enough to do in the Fleet to occupy a family for a good 2-3 hours.** Five flexible exhibit galleries on two levels, a pre-school learning area, an **IMAX® Dome Theater (the Space Theater), and a motion-based simulator ride** comprise the public areas. Take time to look over a handy visitor guide and map in the rotunda before beginning your adventure so you're sure not to miss anything.

The theme of the museum is broad: to increase the public's knowledge of science, technology and the nature of earth and space. Therefore the collection of exhibits is eclectic. On one level, you may find an exhibit that explores the human face; while on another, beautiful photos of the night sky, and on yet another, an Internet weather station. **San Diego's growing importance, as a center for high technology and bioscience research is a key component.**

> On one level, you may find an exhibit that explores the human face; while on another, beautiful photos of the night sky, and on yet another, an Internet weather station.

Designed to immerse the viewer in the action, **the subject matter of IMAX® films available at the Fleet ranges from underwater and outer space spectaculars to land-based explorations of exotic locales such as Everest or Antarctica.** The kids may especially enjoy Comet Impact! This motion-based simulation experience takes 23 people on a short but bumpy space journey to save Earth from an approaching comet. Either this or another science-based scenario will be featured.

The facility is named for an early aerospace industrialist and philanthropist who built many of the bombers used in World War II. He was also the nation's first airmail pilot. Look for a great photo (in Founder's Hall near the Space Theater entrance) of **Major Reuben H. Fleet with President Woodrow Wilson at the dedication of the U.S. airborne mail service.** A generous contribution from his family foundation in the early 1970s made possible the equipping of the original theater/planetarium.

Planetarium shows are not shown on a daily basis. They're presented **every Saturday at 10 a.m. and on the first Wednesday of each month at 7 p.m.** The nighttime shows are followed by hands-on telescope viewing outside near the fountain. These astronomy-based planetarium productions are also shown to school kids on field trips. In addition, the Fleet offers year-round lectures and weekend workshops for all ages on popular science topics.

Of special note is the **Nierman Challenger Learning Center**, a cooperative learning experience simulating a space mission. Classes from fifth grade and up, or corporate groups on a team-building exercise, utilize the second floor facility to complete their mission. The Challenger Center also occasionally offers public missions to the moon and Mars.

Tickets are available for the theater and exhibit galleries or for exhibit galleries only. Tickets for the 23-passenger motion simulator can also be added to any admission package. The center is open every day of the year, and in the evenings on weekends and during the summer. Tickets are available several days in advance at the ticket counter. Advance tickets are recommended for busy weekends. Call for the day's schedule: (619) 238-1233. Or log on to: **www.rhfleet.org**.

San Diego Air and Space Museum

San Diego has made many important contributions to aviation. Therefore it's not surprising that one of the nation's best museums on aviation history is located here. You can't miss the distinctive looking building, nor the content implied by the dramatic exhibits arrayed out front.

As you walk up to the museum, you're greeted by the revolutionary Lockheed A-12 Blackbird spy plane, and the Convair Sea Dart, an experimental seaplane from the 1950s built here in San Diego. Step inside the airy, entry rotunda, and come face to face with the historic Apollo 9 command module, one of only twelve original Apollo spacecraft on public exhibit in the world. Flying above the Apollo is a reproduction of an early hydroplane, the Curtiss A-1. The A-1, the U.S. Navy's first airplane, made its maiden flights in San Diego.

The San Diego Air and Space Museum is actually two museums in one. Entering the exhibit galleries from the rotunda, take time to stroll through the **International Aerospace Hall of Fame-the only one in the world.** Featuring portraits of men and women who have made a major contribution to the advancement of aerospace science, you'll find such legendary names as **Lindbergh, Earhart, Gagarin and Armstrong.** And you'll learn about the extraordinary accomplishments of the world's leading aviation pioneers, pilots, engineers and industrialists.

This is an appropriate introduction to the history of flight that unfolds as you explore the remainder of the museum's large collection. **More than 65 historic aircraft are arrayed in chronological order along a circular gallery**, which surrounds a spacious center courtyard. From the earliest hot-air balloon flights in late 18th-century France to a replica of the cockpit of a space shuttle orbiting high above the earth, you'll be transported to far-off places.

Videos, photographs and models enhance information provided by the larger exhibits throughout the museum. The walkways are so packed with information and displays that you may need to plan a return visit just to take it all in.

There is also a smaller gallery with an impressive exhibition featuring the contributions of **Women in Aviation**, and a 200-seat theater used for special events. Near the end of the gallery spaces is an exciting new addition—the "Planetary Theater." Here visitors will find a globe on which computer controlled images of our planetary neighbors in the solar system are projected. The viewer has the ability to tap into resources from NASA and astronomers and find current detailed information about the planets with the click of a button.

> The San Diego Air and Space Museum is actually two museums in one.

Don't miss the covered courtyard in the center of the museum-the **Pavilion of Flight**. This dramatic space is often rented for private parties, but during the day provides a nice spot to rest your feet while touring the extensive museum. Dedicated to the late Executive Director Edwin McKellar, who led the museum through 20 years of rebuilding its collection after a tragic fire in 1978, the courtyard houses a Vietnam-era Huey Cobra helicopter gunship, a MIG 17, an F4Phantom II, a PBY, and a 1928 Ford Tri-Motor. An historic fountain in the center, if viewed from above, configures a "V-8" symbol-a feature added in 1935 by the Ford Motor Company.

The building was originally designed for the Ford Company as a model manufacturing facility at the 1935 Exposition. The circular galleries replicated an automobile assembly line. Fair-goers walked along the assembly line, and at the end were even invited to "test-drive" newly assembled cars on simulated "Roads of the Pacific." In 1936, the fair's second year, the Ford Building was restyled as the Palace of Transportation. **The *March of Transportation* murals that still adorn the walls were painted at that time by Juan Larrinaga and his assistants.**

Docents give tours of the restoration areas in the huge basement for a modest fee. **Most of the aircraft displayed in the museum are in mint condition** because knowledgeable volunteers have restored them. Many are retired aerospace manufacturing employees. They love to talk about the work they do, and an extra hour spent here will be well remembered.

In addition to the basement restoration area the museum facility **houses an extensive research library for serious students of aviation history.** The museum sponsors year-round children's' educational programs, and a full schedule of activities for members and volunteers. On your way out, **stop by the Museum Store for great books on aviation history, flight jackets, NASA patches, and of course scale models** that can be built at home.

The museum is located at the south end of Pan American Plaza, adjacent to the Automotive Museum and Starlight Bowl. One of the most popular museums in the Park, it is open daily from 10 a.m. to 4:30 p.m. (5:30 p.m. between Memorial Day and Labor Day), except Thanksgiving, Christmas and New Year's Day. Call (619) 234-8291 for further information, or log on to: **www.airandspace.org**.

San Diego Art Institute: Museum of the Living Artist

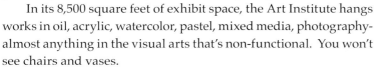

The San Diego Art Institute, its entrance tucked modestly under the arcade on the north side of the House of Charm, is **one of the Park's best-kept secrets**.

Behind its low profile is a **splendid little gallery dedicated to displaying and advancing the work of regional artists**. The closest thing San Diego has to a municipal gallery, the institute **shows more than 3,000 works each year.** If pressed for time, you can do this gallery in half an hour.

In its 8,500 square feet of exhibit space, the Art Institute hangs works in oil, acrylic, watercolor, pastel, mixed media, photography- almost anything in the visual arts that's non-functional. You won't see chairs and vases.

All work displayed at the Art Institute is less than two years old. The organization supports the living-artist community by offering opportunity for exposure and exhibition of regional visual arts. This philosophy is carried out through programs which include the highly successful regional juried shows, displaying about

100 pieces, most of which can be purchased. The jurors, who are art educators or certified authorities, select the exhibitions from works hand-delivered by local artists. Juried shows change every four to six weeks.

The juried shows occupy most of the museum space, but the youth gallery and the intriguing "one-foot show" are not to be missed. You'll find the latter in the northwest corner. No piece can be larger than one foot In any direction, and some of the intricate works are a good deal smaller. Single artists are regularly showcased in various exhibits of 20 to 25 pieces.

In cooperation with the California Art Educators Association, the Institute displays works of students from kindergarten through 12th grade in the **David G. Fleet Youth Gallery.** This space is doubled during **Youth Art Month**, mid-January to mid-February, when a much greater number of works from San Diego City and County schools are shown. Meanwhile, various classes and workshops are held for all ages at a site on Kettner Boulevard, several blocks west of the Park.

Special exhibitions are held at various times. A Southern California Awards Exhibition takes place every fall and an international awards show is held in the spring. Another popular event is the semiannual **"C-Note Show,"** held in late June and during **Balboa Park December Nights**, the first weekend in December. Art fanciers snap up some good deals at the C-Note Show, where every item is for sale at **$100, $200 or $300**.

The gift shop, right at the entrance, sells only works by regional artists (even the greeting cards) except for logo items such as T-shirts, caps and tote bags.

The Institute is open from 10 a.m. to 4 p.m. Tuesday through Saturday, and noon to 4 p.m. on Sunday. Admission for adults, seniors and college students is inexpensive. Children under 12 are free. It's closed on most holidays. For more information on classes or workshops, call (619) 236-0011. The Web address is **www.sandiego-art.org.**

San Diego Automotive Museum

If you like classic cars and motorcycles or simply appreciate the master craftsmanship of years gone by, you'll love the San Diego Automotive Museum.

Bentleys, Rolls-Royces, Cadillacs, Packards and Pierce-Arrows, all in mint condition, vie for the eye along with Ford "Woodies," a 1948 Tucker "Torpedo," and a large collection of motorcycles. These include Harley Davidson, Indian, Salisbury, Norton and Triumph bikes.

One of the first things you'll see is a replica of Oscar's Drive-In, a popular San Diego hangout of the 1950s, occupying the north wall to your right. Cars from special exhibits are placed there, making it an ideal setting to show off styling and design.

Although the museum owns a large number of vintage vehicles, **private collectors contribute to the rotating displays**, which change at least four times a year.

> If you like classic cars and motorcycles or simply appreciate the master craftsmanship of years gone by, you'll love the San Diego Automotive Museum.

The **motorcycle collection includes a one-of-its-kind 1942 Harley Davidson with a sidecar on the left, built in Canada for World War II use in England**. It's the only one still in existence. The Engine Room displays, among others, a 1906 Stanley steam engine and the air-cooled engine of a 1924 Franklin.

Museum vehicles not on exhibit are stored in a warehouse/ workshop in National City (not open to the public) where volunteer mechanics and autobody specialists restore them.

The museum has an educational function as well as displaying classic vehicles. Field trips are offered to San Diego schools and other educational institutions throughout the county. In addition, students from local colleges and universities are offered the opportunity to participate in an internship program, earning academic credit and valuable experience.

The **Richard A. Teague Research Library** contains automotive histories, biographies, vintage owner's manuals, rare photos, and a large collection of Road and Track, Antique Motor News, Auto Age and other periodicals. You may use the resource center the first time at no charge. For additional visits, you'll need to buy a museum membership (starting at $30 for an individual.)

A **Racing Hall of Fame, occupying the south part of the mezzanine, honors such auto racing greats as Juan Fangio, Carroll Shelby, Rodger Ward, Phil Hill and Parnelli Jones**.

One of the museum's outreach programs is a cooperative venture with the R.J. Donovan Correctional Facility. Often on display is a Canadian-built 1924 McLaughlin-Buick, beautifully restored by prison inmates.

Books, models, posters and other items from automotive history are available in the museum store. Call (619) 231-2886 or check out their colorful Web site: **www.sdautomuseum.org**.

San Diego Hall of Champions Sports Museum

The San Diego Hall of Champions went from being a very nice regional sports museum to an interactive, 21st Century educational center when it reopened in 1999 in the Park's Palisades area.

Located in the handsomely renovated Federal Building, the Hall of Champions now **has more than 40,000 square feet of exhibit space**-in which to honor hometown heroes in more than 40 sports, display traveling and permanent exhibits, and showcase its many amenities. Start by picking up a self-guided tour booklet, which profiles and maps all the features on the Hall's three levels.

Founded half a century ago by civic leader Robert Breitbard, the Hall of Champions still honors local Stars of the Month and Stars of the Year dating to the 1940s. Legendary members of the Breitbard Hall of Fame include baseball's Ted Williams, football's Terrell Davis and America's Cup victor Dennis Conner. The San Diego Chargers' Hall of Fame is also located here. Besides these points of interest, there are a number of high-tech and interactive goodies, including a state-of-the-art research center, and a theater for viewing classic sports films and tapes. There is even a broadcasters' booth where you are able to choose your sport and call the play-by-play action. Other exhibits are planned to fill in the museum's vast spaces.

In the Hall of Champions' **state-of-the-art education resource center** (the word "library" isn't adequate) students of sport can view thousands of digitized photographs, conduct research electronically, and link online to sports sites around the world.

You can take a seventh-inning stretch and slake your hunger or thirst at the **Time-Out Cafe**, and load up on various sports souvenirs at The **Store of Champion**s. Sports artists often display their paintings, many of which can be purchased, on the lower level near the Archives Room. Sports memorabilia and artwork can be purchased in the Store of Champions or on their Web site.

The Walter J. Zable Banquet Room, with a smashing view of Balboa Park and part of San Diego Bay, is available for group luncheons or dinner meetings along with several other rooms. The entire museum may also be rented for private events. Phone: (619) 234-2544 or log on to: **www.sdhoc.org**.

San Diego Model Railroad Museum

The San Diego Model Railroad Museum **has the largest permanent operating scale model and toy train display in the United States**. The 24,000-square-foot museum contains four enormous scale-model layouts, which depict railroads of the Southwest in O, HO and N scales, including an "HO" 1/87 actual size replica of one of the largest timber trestles in North America. Over the years, **volunteer model railroad enthusiasts have painstakingly created a very special environment, down to the minutest detail**. (The museum offers a list of interesting and humorous things to look for in the dioramas; ask at the admissions desk.) Today volunteers from four different local model railroad clubs take turns running the trains and delight in sharing their avocation with visitors. The Toy Train Gallery has hands-on throttles for children and operating toy trains of Lionel O-Gauge.

Now proudly accredited by the American Association of Museums (one of only 60 museums in California), the museum also **features permanent and visiting exhibits of railroad artifacts**. Located on the lower level in the Casa de Balboa. Open Tuesday-Friday, 11 a.m. to 4 p.m.; Saturday and Sunday, 11 a.m. to 5 p.m. Low-priced admission fees for adults and seniors 55 and over, students and active duty military; children under 15 free. **Themed gift shop**. Public Information (619) 696-0199; Web address: **www.sdmrm.org**.

San Diego Museum of Art

Before entering the Museum of Art, take a moment to admire its **remarkable Spanish Renaissance facade**. Faces and statues will stare down at you, including those of the great painters Velasquez and El Greco.

Once inside, you'll face a formal entry rotunda dominated by a fountain donated by the John and Sally Thornton Foundation.

Beyond that are 36,665 square feet of exhibit space arranged in **18 galleries on two floors**. There's also an **outdoor Sculpture Garden** west of the museum proper, which you can enter free from the Plaza de Panama. Its large-scale 20th century works include a **Rodin** and a **Henry Moore**.

Allow two hours or more to enjoy the museum, which has made itself quite visitor-friendly to Spanish speakers through its bilingual wall texts, brochures and presentations.

The permanent collection contains 12,000 holdings and continues to grow. Major gifts include a collection of 100 works by Toulouse-Lautrec. You can look up any artist or painting in the museum's collection in the computer gallery on the first floor.

Among the best pieces are those in the Asian collection, displayed on the ground level just west of the rotunda. Among the frequently rotting works In the Asian Court, the museum features earthenware vessels from the Shang Dynasty, stoneware and pottery from the Sung Dynasty, and rare calligraphy by prominent Chinese political figures, including Chiang Kai-shek. A sculpted pair of Shinto guardian deities of the 16th century highlights the Japanese collection. Important European paintings include **oils by El Greco, Goya, Rubens, and an early Monet**. Works from the 19th to early 20th century are hung in the ground floor rooms adjacent to the rotunda and the Asian collection. **American art** is also displayed on the first floor. **European art from the Baroque period** is displayed primarily on the second floor.

You can hear a free (with your paid admission) docent-led tour of the galleries daily. Check the schedule near the Thornton Fountain in the rotunda for specific times (generally 11 a.m. and 1 p.m.)

The museum regularly hosts traveling exhibits that remain for up to four months. Recent examples are: "Degas in Bronze: The Complete Sculptures;" and "St. Peter and the Vatican: The Legacy of the Popes."

Outreach and education programs include: night classes for adults and children; the Museum Art School for ages 4 through 18; free quarterly **Family Festivals**, with special activities related to specific exhibitions; and **annual Summer Art Camps** for schoolchildren. These are co-ed day camps for ages 6 to 18. To sign up, call the museum's Education Department, (619) 231-1996. For information on free lectures and special events, call (619) 696-1966.

The **museum store**, adjacent to the rotunda as you enter, **offers cards, posters, art books** and **some small art works**. Also featured is artistically designed and handmade jewelry by the world's most original designers.

Snack and full luncheon menu service are available just outside the museum entrance at **Waters Café @ SDMA**. Lunch in the elegant courtyard is served amidst some of the outdoor sculptures.

Museum hours are 10 a.m. to 6 p.m. Tuesday through Sunday, and until 9 p.m. on Thursdays. Ticket prices begin at $10 for adults and $4 for youngsters (6 to 17), with discounts for seniors (65+), active military, and college students; admission is free for children under 6. For national blockbuster exhibits, prices may be higher than usual. Phone: (619) 232-7931. The Web address is **www.sdmart.org.**

San Diego Museum of Man

If you're intrigued by mankind's beginnings, and our earliest tools, weapons, pottery and textiles-or if you just think ancient mummies are cool-the **San Diego Museum of Man** is well worth a visit. Located just off Cabrillo Bridge at the Park's west entrance, San Diego's only **anthropological museum has a collection of artifacts, folk art and archaeological finds** so vast (more than 75,000 items) that only five to 10 percent are on display at any one time.

The museum sits beneath **two landmarks**, the Park's signature **California Tower and an exquisitely-tiled Moorish dome**. On the exterior of the large tiled dome are the following words (from Deuteronomy 8:8, appearing in Latin): "A land of wheat and barley and vines and fig trees and pomegranates-a land of olive oil and honey." This phrase was considered an apt description of California by Exposition planners. The structure was built to house the State of California's exhibits for the 1915 Panama-California Exposition. With two overhead passageways, it's the only building to span El Prado with exhibit space on each side of the street.

> The structure was built to house the State of California's exhibits for the 1915 Panama-California Expostion.

Once inside, take a moment to admire the 90-square-foot Palenque and Yacxchilan bas relief panels on the entryway's side walls. Straight ahead, a 26-foot Guatemelan stela, or column, towers impressively skyward. **This exhibit, which dates back to the 1915 Exposition**, has recently been restored and put back on display. Walking toward it be sure to stop and look straight up at the underside of the huge Moorish dome 80 feet above your head.

Permanent exhibits include genuine **ancient Egyptian mummies, native Californian and Southwestern art, and many more visual feasts.** The museum creates displays from among its huge collection and also assembles traveling exhibits. **"Footsteps in Time"** is an especially noteworthy $2 million permanent exhibit on human evolution that was **funded, in part, by the National Science Foundation**.

At the hands-on **Children's Discovery Center** on the second floor, kids can get a sense of Ancient Egypt's 18th Dynasty as they pretend to barter in an Egyptian market, dress the "Royal Cat" and don the robes of a pharaoh, a scribe, or a princess. Here they can enter a "Tomb Room" to sit on a royal throne, see a pretend mummy, and write her a message. Kids and adults alike can play a game called Senet, and learn about modern-day archaeology in Egypt.

Educational programs include a teachers' resource center, assistance to scholars and researchers, a forensics workshop for local police forces, student internships and docent programs. **Lectures, films and symposia are frequently presented.** The museum conducts three annual cultural awareness programs: **Indian Fair, Conversations in Culture, and a Swedish Christmas.** The museum has also recently begun offering a regular cultural event called "Tower After Hours" showcasing the music and food of a different country each month.

A lovely gift store offers native and mesoamerican arts and crafts, Egyptian jewelry and sculptures, and more than 600 book titles. The museum's elegant **St. Francis Chapel** is one of the Park's best secrets. This replica of a chapel in Tetotzotlán, Mexico, may be reserved for a wedding or other special use, but is not open for general viewing.

The Park's **famed carillon perches high above in the California Tower**, faithfully chiming out the time every quarter hour. On Fridays at noon and on certain holidays, you may also hear a 15-minute concert of seasonal music from the carillon float across the Park.

The museum is open daily from 10 to 4:30, except Thanksgiving, Christmas and New Years. An entrance fee is charged. Annual family, individual and student memberships provide free museum admission, extra passes for others, and discounts on lectures, special events and items in the museum store. For more information, call (619) 239-2001. The Web site is **www.museumofman.org**.

San Diego Natural History Museum

The third oldest scientific institution west of the Mississippi, located just north of the big fountain at the east end of the Prado, was vastly expanded at the turn of this century.

The **Natural History Museum focuses on the habitats of Southern California and Baja California, with exhibits illustrating the geology, biology, geography and climate zones of this highly diverse region**. More than 7.5 million specimens comprise the museum's permanent collection.

A recent $26 million expansion of 90,000 square feet has more than doubled the facility's size, with a large exhibit hall, a 300-seat giant-screen theater, a stunning atrium, and a new, north-facing entrance. Permanent and traveling exhibits popular with school children and adults draw more than 300,000 visitors a year to the museum. Large shows on dinosaurs have made several appearances. **A spectacular multi-million dollar permanent exhibit entitled "Fossil Mysteries" opened in 2006**, exploring the San Diego region over eons—back as far as they have fossil evidence-some three to four million years ago.

The museum has many research and education partnerships with Mexican scientists. Its traveling exhibit "Desert and Sea: Visions of Baja California" has been extensively shown in Mexico, while the content of the giant-screen film, "Ocean Oasis," developed with the help of Mexican science advisors, contributed to the recent naming of the Sea of Cortez as a World Heritage Site (UNESCO).

The **Environmental Science Education Center** offers a vast array of comprehensive programs for all ages. These range from on-site lectures, children's classes and summer camps, to exotic field trips to the Arctic (to see polar bears), Baja (whales and rock art) and even France (prehistoric caves and medieval castles). Some are for members only.

Admission is charged with senior, military, student and group discounts available. Family, individual, senior and student memberships are also available, with benefits including free admission, passes for friends, pre-exhibit parties, insider lectures and discounts on store items. Films shown in the large-format theater are included with admission; usually two different films are offered on an alternating basis, with up to six screenings daily. Special events and receptions can be held throughout the museum, including the building's rooftop, with a grand view of Florida Canyon as a backdrop. Up to 2,000 people can be accommodated.

There's both **a museum store with a wide variety of gift items on the main floor and a smaller shop on the lower level** which is open for special exhibits. Museum hours are 10 a.m. to 5 p.m. all year. For information, call (619) 232-3821. The Web address is **www.sdnhm.org**.

San Diego Zoo—in a class by itself

It's probably not fair to lump the world-famous San Diego Zoo in with all the other cultural institutions, but after all it is in Balboa Park. The Zoo is one of the City's most popular attractions with well **over 3 million visitors annually**. In fact, the San Diego Zoo, best known for its animals, is actually a 100-acre "park **within a park"—with a botanical collection of more than 6,500 plant species** that has earned accreditation from the American Association of Museums.

It's not surprising that the Zoo is so popular. People are endlessly fascinated by colorful, exotic animals, and the Zoological Society of San Diego has a well-deserved reputation as a leader in the field of animal conservation and education.

The Zoo had its origins in the 1915-16 Exposition, like so many of the facilities on the Park's Central Mesa. Exposition Surgeon Dr. Harry Wegeforth, enchanted by the exotic animals brought to San Diego for the fair, lobbied the City to become their caretaker, promoted the idea of a zoo in San Diego, and subsequently founded the Zoological Society. He is also responsible for planting and cultivating many of the exotic plants seen throughout the grounds. As did Kate Sessions, he collected cuttings and seeds during his world travels, for beautifying Park grounds.

The tropical foliage, walk-through aviaries and other attractive enclosures, meandering paths, and mysterious bird and animal calls you hear in the background delight the senses. **With the botanical collection and more than 800 species and 4,000 animals to see, you could easily spend several days at the Zoo alone**. Most likely you only have a few hours. With some resourceful planning it is possible to see a good bit of the Zoo in a short amount of time.

If you only have a few hours to spend at the Zoo...

Purchase the "**Best Value**" ticket package (Hint: look for discounts in hotel brochure racks or at the Balboa Park Visitors Center), and take the guided double-deck bus tour when you first arrive (near the Zoo entrance). This will give you a good overview of the exhibits and orientation to the layout of the grounds.

The driver delivers an entertaining and informative commentary along the way. Afterwards go back and visit the areas that most interest you. If koalas and pandas are your thing, you'll know how to find them, and will already have tips for viewing that day.

If you're not afraid of heights and like to hike a bit, take the **Skyfari aerial tram** system across the Zoo to **Hoof & Horn Mesa** (just about the farthest point), and hike back. The tree-top views of the Park and downtown San Diego are breathtaking, and it's usually cool and quiet up there. (Roundtrip Skyfari vouchers are included in the "Best value" admission package.)

On the way back, take advantage of the escalators available on steep hillsides whenever possible. (One that will save you much walking is located near the panda enclosure. Stop mid-way and visit the **Asian Rainforest Aviary**.)

The best time of day to visit is early in the morning—the animals are more active, and you can sometimes watch them interact with the keepers. Coming right at 9 a.m. when the Zoo opens is a good way to avoid midday heat and large crowds.

This is also probably your best bet to see the popular giant pandas without a long wait. *But take the bus tour first* to get oriented. The popular giant panda enclosure opens at 10 a.m., so let the first crush of visitors get their glimpse of the much-publicized baby, and plan to arrive about 45 minutes later. (Don't be disappointed, though, if you don't get a good view of the latest baby panda—look for a hint on the best way to view the newest baby panda at the end of this section.)

Or follow the lead of one frequent Zoo visitor and instead head to **Polar Bear Plunge.** These magnificent animals are usually quite frisky and playful in the morning when the outside temperature is lower. Watch them push off from the underwater glass barrier as they play an energetic game of catch with a plastic ball.

The quickest way to get to the Polar Bear Plunge exhibit is to take the Skyfari aerial tram, boarding near the **Reptile House**, just past the Zoo exit. Purchase tickets for the aerial tram and double-deck bus tours at the Tours & Tickets Booth adjacent to Flamingo Lagoon, across from the main entrance.

An exciting new exhibit, "**Absolutely Apes**," opened in 2005, for the first time enabling Indonesian orangutans and siamangs to occupy the same habitat; "**Monkey Trails**" followed in 2006. These two popular enclaves are near the main entrance.

The Zoo offers guided, behind-the-scenes tours for a fee. These 2½ hour tours, available for individuals and groups of 15 or more, are designed for ages 12 and up. Call (619) 557-3962 for an individual tour reservation; (619) 675-7900 for a group.

If you have the whole day to spend at the Zoo...

Plan to have a special lunch at **Albert's in the Gorilla Tropics area**. This full-service restaurant and bar, located on the lower level in the **Treehouse complex**, features a very good menu at fairly reasonable prices. Its tropical atmosphere is guaranteed to restore your spirits for the rest of the afternoon. You can make a reservation in advance by calling (619) 685-3200.

On a budget? Also in the same complex is a cafeteria-style restaurant—**the Treehouse Café**—where you can purchase hot entrees and sandwiches and carry them outside to a deck perched **high above the tree-tops of Cat Canyon**.

Hint: Head for seating on the lower level deck of the Treehouse Café with your tray—it's less crowded and feels more like a real tree house—look for steps down from the main seating deck near the restaurant entrance.

There are too many wonderful attractions at the San Diego Zoo to mention them all, but don't miss **Ituri Forest** (African rainforest exhibit) with its charming river otters and small primates; **Hippo Beach** (especially in the late afternoon or early evening); and **Tiger River** nearby. Off the beaten path, but other "must-sees," especially if you have children in your party, are the walk-in **hummingbird aviary** and the **Children's Zoo** with its **animal babies' nursery**.

The Zoo is open 365 days a year at 9 a.m. Most of the year, the gates close at 4 p.m., but visitors may stay on the grounds until 5 or 6 p.m. In summer, the **Nighttime Zoo** offers a special opportunity to stay on the grounds until 10 p.m. (gates close at 9 p.m.) The Zoo is open free on the first Monday in October, **Founders Day**. Needless to say, Balboa Park and the Zoo are jammed on this day, as thousands turn out for the big event.

Catered events on the Zoo grounds are available for groups of 70 or more: call (619) 718-3020. **Year-round education programs are available for all ages.** Reservations are required: call (619) 557-3969.

For current schedule and admission prices, call (619) 234-3153. TDD: (619) 233-9639. **Membership in the Zoological Society** is one of the best bargains in San Diego as it includes unlimited admission to the Zoo and the Wild Animal Park near Escondido and several guest passes (restrictions apply). For membership info, call (619) 231-0251.

Hint: For information on all of the above, or to view the pandas live, 24 hours a day, log on to **www.sandiegozoo.org**, like millions of fans around the world.

Spanish Village Art Center

During the second exposition, this area was devoted to small shops, with the buildings **made to look like a typical Spanish village**. When the fair was over, the village was scheduled for demolition, but citizens asked that the buildings be used as an artists' colony. As a result, the Spanish Village Art Center, Inc., was formed and occupied the studios until 1942. During the war, Spanish Village was the only area of the Park to be used by the Army. Much damage resulted during the military's use and later by vandals. After some repairs, the artist group was allowed to resume occupancy and continue the restoration. It has now been declared an historic site.

There are currently 37 studios where over 50 artists and crafts-people demonstrate their skills and techniques in painting, sculpture, photography, jewelry, stained glass, enamel, the lapidary arts, woodcarving, glass blowing, and pottery. Original art works are offered for sale. Various guilds housed in the Village present art shows on the flagstone patio, where food and entertainment are also offered. Gallery 21 has bimonthly shows featuring various media. Spanish Village Art Center Is open seven days a week and the admission Is free. Public information (619) 233-9050 or log onto **www.spanishvillageart.com**.

> **Hint:** Not inside, but just to the east of Spanish Village, at 1721 Village Place, is a small **Photo Arts Building** (not to be confused with the Museum of Photographic Arts on page 86). The Southern California Association of Camera Clubs operates out of this facility, which is only open noon to 4 p.m. on Sundays and on Saturdays during the month of June, July and August. Ten camera clubs also use the building for regular meetings. For more information, visit **www.sdacc.us** or call (619) 232-1321.

Timken Museum of Art

You can't miss this small museum on the northeast corner of Plaza de Panama, for it's one of the few buildings in the Park without a trace of Spanish-influenced architecture. Whether you think the Italian marble and bronze structure is an eclectic enhancement to the Park or an unfortunate aberration, the interior is a jewel.

If you're pressed for time but want to experience some marvelous paintings, the 5,000-square-foot Timken can be enjoyed in less than an hour- and it's always free.

The Timken's has an outstanding collection of European "Old Master" paintings, American paintings, and Russian icons. Almost all the museum's 50 paintings are on permanent display in the galleries. The museum's collection includes Rembrandt's "Saint Bartholomew" which the master painted in 1637. Recently cleaned and restored, many of his subtle, dark brush strokes are visible or the first time in years.

Entering the Timken, which has never charged admission, you'll first come to the rotunda, dominated by a sculpture of Mercury by Giovanni da Bologna. The work is a 19th Century casting of the original Bologna masterwork and is flanked by 18-foot-high French tapestries from the 16th century.

The Timken's six galleries are arranged around the rotunda and are home to the museum's permanent collection of Spanish, Dutch, Flemish and American paintings and one of the most extensive collections of Russian religious icons in the United States. The intricate icons are all panel paintings, applied on door and shutter-like wood panels.

Skylights provide natural light for viewing. Three layers of filtering glass block ultraviolet light that can harm the paintings, electric lights being switched on only on cloudy days. The museum's architect, Frank L. Hope, studied lighting and climate control in other museums and consulted with top lighting engineers before designing the Timken in 1965.

Two special exhibitions are shown each year, often built around one of the paintings. Education is a key part of the Timken's programming, and the museum regularly hosts school groups from around San Diego and neighboring Baja California. The Timken was the first museum in the Park to establish a core of Spanish-speaking docents. The museum works closely with other galleries throughout the region and has loaned select pieces of its collection for exhibitions at the Tijuana Cultural Center.

> If you're pressed for time but want to experience some marvelous paintings, the 5,000-square-foot Timken can be enjoyed in less than an hour— and it's always free.

A legacy of San Diego art patrons Anne and Amy Putnam, whose collection now resides at the museum, the Timken opened in 1965 with substantial funding from **the Timken Foundation of Ohio**.

The museum is closed throughout September for maintenance and a thorough survey of its holdings. The rest of the year, the museum is open from 10 a.m. to 4:30 p.m. Tuesday through Saturday, and from 1:30 to 4:30 p.m. on Sunday. The museum offers longer hours in the summer and provides a regular series of lectures, discussions and special programs related to its collection and exhibitions. Docent-guided tours can be arranged by contacting the museum. Admission is always free. Call (619) 239-5548 for more information. The Web site is **www.timkenmuseum.org**

United Nations Association of San Diego

The United Nations Building houses the United Nations Association of San Diego (UNA-SD) and the San Diego Committeee for UNICEF, the Eleanor Roosevelt Global Classroom, and a unique **International Gift Shop**. UNA-SD is a non-profit educational organization dedicated to strengthening public understanding and support for international cooperation through the United Nations. UNA-SD's office hours are Monday-Friday, 11 a.m. to 3 p.m.

The International Gift Shop provides financial support for the UNA-SD through the sale of unique world handicrafts including international candies, jewelry, books, toys, and gifts as well as world music. A special hand-painted alcove in the gift shop and two large murals in the classroom were commissioned to honor the work of UNICEF on behalf of children the world over. Open daily 10 a.m. to 4:30 p.m.

The building originally housed the Christian Science Monitor Exhibit for the second Expo in 1935. Camera enthusiasts began used the building until 1942, when the Navy took over most of the Park. In 1948, the building was returned to the Photo Arts Group, which remained there until 1960. **Former First Lady Eleanor Roosevelt helped lobby the San Diego City Council to find a permanent home for the United Nations Association in Balboa Park**. Located in the House of Hospitality from 1953, the Association moved in on July 1, 1960.   Ph: UNA-SD (619) 233-3970; Gift Shop (619) 233-5044. To reach UNICEF, call (619) 233-8457.

Veterans Museum and Memorial Center

The Veterans Museum and Memorial Center honors and perpetuates the memory of all men and women who have served in the U.S. armed forces, Coast Guard or wartime Merchant Marine. Programs are offered which promote public awareness of the contributions of these veterans and their relationship to San Diego. A variety of **historical artifacts, documents, memorabilia and artwork dating from the Civil War through the Gulf War** are on display-some of it very moving. Large murals depict key events and involvement of San Diego veterans.

The center is located in the former Balboa Naval Hospital Chapel at Inspiration Point on the east side of Park Boulevard. It provides facilities for memorial services and meetings, receptions, dinners, and ceremonies of all kinds for veterans, active duty military personnel, and the general public. **More than three dozen San Diego veterans groups meet there, including the United Veterans Council.** A memorial service is conducted at 11:30 a.m. on the fourth Saturday of each month honoring the area's recently deceased veterans.

Don't miss the beautiful reflecting pool, scale-model statue of a B-24 Liberator (these planes were originally built in San Diego) and peaceful views of the city out front in the garden, which will eventually honor veterans who have fought in the air, and on land and sea. The first portion, the Air Garden, is now complete.

The Veterans Museum is open from 9:30 a.m. to 3 p.m., Tuesday through Saturday. Admission is free but donations are most welcome. Public information: (619) 239-2300. Web site: **www.veteranmuseum.org**.

Veterans War Memorial Building

In August 1947, the Park Commission approved the construction of a $300,000 War Memorial Building on the western edge of the Indian Village site (from the 1915 Exposition). The building was **dedicated almost 60 years ago as a memorial** "to our honored dead of all wars and to the Americans who have fought for the four freedoms." It has six meeting rooms and an auditorium. Eight veterans' organizations meet there, including the Fleet Reserve

Association and the Disabled American Veterans. The building also houses the **City's Therapeutic Recreation Services** program and the Park and Recreation Department's training division. Also using the building are numerous non-veteran organizations.

WorldBeat Center

The WorldBeat Center opened in Balboa Park in September 1996. Like the nearby Centro Cultural de la Raza, it is **housed in a former water tower**, which, prior to 1996, served as an equipment storage area. It is operated by WorldBeat Productions, established in 1980 and incorporated in 1985 as a **non-profit multicultural arts organization** dedicated to the promotion and presentation of African and other Third World traditional styles, as well as contemporary American art, music and dance derived from these influences. **Dozens of dance and drumming classes for all ages** are offered year-round. Hours vary. Public Information: (619) 230-1190 or visit their colorful Web site: **www.worldbeatcenter.org**

BALBOA PARK AND THE LIVELY (PERFORMING) ARTS
by Charlene Baldridge

Even before fan dancer Sally Rand stirred the breeze back in 1935, Balboa Park had an association with the performing arts by virtue of its use as an entertainment destination during the two expositions, the Panama-California Exposition of 1915-16 and California Pacific International Exposition of 1935-36.

The Spreckels Organ was created to herald the 1915 Expo in music, and one of the loveliest theater complexes in the world, The Old Globe, traces its roots to performances during the 1935-1936 fair.

Those who planned the California Pacific International Exposition invited several entertainment attractions popular at the 1934 Chicago World's Fair to repeat their success in San Diego, among them Rand. They also engaged the Globe Players, a company of young professionals, to perform 50-minute versions of William Shakespeare's plays.

While Rand titillated audiences, folks bent on another kind of entertainment thrilled to the Globe Players' truncated versions of such works as *Hamlet, Much Ado About Nothing,* and *The Taming of the Shrew,* performed in an open-to-the-sky theater, modeled after Shakespeare's original London Globe.

Old Globe Theatre

Scheduled for demolition at the close of the Expo in 1936, the Globe and its outbuildings were saved from the wrecking ball and purchased by a group of civic-minded community actors, who raised funds for the renovation and upgrading needed to bring them into compliance with building codes of the time.

San Diego's Old Globe Theatre, opened as a community theater in 1937, currently plays to approximately 250,000 people annually. If one includes the 1935-36 fair, audiences saw nearly 700 productions during the Old Globe's first 65 years.

Recipient of a 1984 Special Tony Award for "notable past achievements and continuing dedication to theater artistry," the Old Globe operates under a year-round contract with Actors' Equity Association. In addition to an annual holiday show, the organization **presents 12 or more productions each year** in three intimate theaters, the 225-seat Cassius Carter Center Stage, the 581-seat Old Globe Theatre, and the 612-seat outdoor Lowell Davies Festival Theatre.

In addition to Shakespeare, which is produced in the summer, audiences enjoy **beautifully produced classical works as well as musicals and contemporary plays** that may include world pre-mieres. Among works premiered at the Old Globe and later seen on Broadway are Stephen Sondheim's *Into the Woods,* Neil Simon's *Rumors* and *Jake's Women,* and Terrence McNally's *The Full Monty.*

Among the renowned artists who have acted on Globe stages are Angela Bassett, Charles S. Dutton, Laurence Fishburne, John Goodman, Hal Holbrook, Cherry Jones, Bebe Neuwirth, Christopher Reeve, Marion Ross, Christopher Walken and James Whitmore.

The playgoing experience is enhanced by the beauty of the Old Globe's setting between the Museum of Man, the San Diego Museum of Art and the San Diego Zoo. The theaters are grouped around a handsomely laid out plaza. **Pre-theater food and**

beverages may be purchased at the pub and eaten at one of its charming outdoor tables. Theatrically-themed gifts are available at the gift shop.

In the Festival Theatre on a summer evening, audiences are surrounded by towering eucalyptus trees, and the forest behind the stage frequently becomes a part of the theatrical experience, along with ambient noise from the Zoo.

Behind-the-scenes tours (of all three stages as well as the costume and scenery workshops) are available for a modest fee most Saturdays and Sundays at 10:30 a.m. Call for information and reservations. Phone: (619) 231-1941; box office, (619) 239-2255; Web site: **www.oldglobe.org**.

San Diego Civic Light Opera

The San Diego Civic Light Opera Association (**Starlight Musical Theatre**) was founded in 1945 and produced Gilbert and Sullivan's *Mikado* in Wegeforth Bowl at the San Diego Zoo the following year. Other early productions included *The Chocolate Soldier, H.M.S. Pinafore,* and *Naughty Marietta*.

Over the course of 60 subsequent seasons, now presented at the 4,200-seat Starlight Bowl during the summer months, audiences totaling four million enjoyed nearly 1,000 performances of 120 musicals. Generations of San Diegans have been raised on and enamored of the Starlight tradition.

The Starlight experience is a family affair that begins early in the evening-in order to secure the best picnic spot and enjoy a leisurely meal prior to curtain.

Located off President's Way on Pan American Plaza, **the bowl is surrounded by grassy areas suitable for dining al fresco.** Favorite spots are near the House of Pacific Relations, the rolling lawn at the corner of Park Blvd. and President's Way, and the areas adjacent to and behind the Air and Space Museum.

Some groups dine formally, toting tables, tablecloths, candles, and champagne flutes. Others spread blankets on the grass and eat home-fried chicken, potato salad, and all the traditional trimmings. Food is also available for purchase near the box office.

However one dines, the musical is truly the thing. Among the most produced Starlight musicals are *The King and I, Kiss Me, Kate, My Fair Lady, The Music Man, Oklahoma, Show Boat, The Sound of Music* and *South Pacific*. Close on their heels in frequency of production are *Brigadoon, Carousel, Camelot* and *Fiddler on the Roof.*

Starlight's innovative "stop-action" is the solution to its location right under the Lindbergh Field flight landing approach. This innovation has earned Starlight international notoriety. A plane spotter alerts the musical's conductor and performers to a plane's approach through a series of lights: yellow for caution, potential freeze; red for freeze action; and green for resume the show. To the delight of audiences, action could and does freeze during climactic moments.

Starlight casts Actors Equity performers in leading roles, then fills out the company with semi-professional and amateur performers, some drawn from its own apprentice program, instituted in 1970. Phone: (619) 544-7827. Web Site: **www. starlighttheatre.org.**

Balboa Park Puppet Guild

What is now the 234-seat Marie Hitchcock Puppet Theater was originally part of the Palisades Building, a single, large unit built for the California Pacific International Exposition that was split into three separate spaces following World War II.

The first public performance at the Puppet Theater was a marionette show given by Marie Hitchcock and her sister, Genevieve Engman. Sponsored by the San Diego Park and Recreation Department, the sisters presented shows at the theater during summer months and in December, an activity Hitchcock continued until she died in 1994.

Marie Hitchcock Puppet Theater

The Balboa Park Puppet Guild began sponsoring a regular summer performance series in 1964, and in 1983 began offering year-round performances. In 1994, the schedule was expanded again to include weekday performances.

Today, **performances are scheduled Wednesday through Sunday**, with added shows on Saturday and Sunday. Visit the Balboa Park Visitors Center for a schedule, or phone the Balboa Park Puppet Guild hotline at (619) 280-8598 or log on at: **www. balboaparkpuppets.com**

San Diego Junior Theatre

Known as the oldest youth theater program in the United States, the San Diego Junior Theatre was established in 1948 by Craig Noel, at the time, resident director of the Old Globe Theatre. During the 1950s, the Junior Theatre operated under the aegis of the Civic Conservatory for Youth. It became fully independent in 1964. **Performances take place year round in the 640-seat Casa del Prado Theater**, which is located just south of the Zoo entrance off Village Place.

Over its five-decade existence, the **Junior Theatre has launched the careers of several well-known actors**. One of its first productions was *The Rose and the Ring*, which featured Dennis Hopper, then an apprentice actor at the Old Globe Theatre. Screen actor Raquel Welch danced in *Caribbean Holiday* in 1955, and Broadway musical star Brian Stokes Mitchell, who won a 2000 Tony Award for Best Performance by a Leading Actor in a Musical (*Kiss Me, Kate*) played the leading role in *Bye-Bye Birdie* in 1978.

The Junior Theatre audience consists largely of families with young children. The six annual mainstage **productions are a mix of contemporary and classic musicals and plays**, among them works written specifically for children. Each season strives for a mixture that is likely to include a Broadway musical, a Shakespeare play, and perhaps even a work by Charles Dickens.

In addition to performance opportunities for youth ages 8 through 18, the Junior Theatre provides **one of the largest children's theater education programs in the United States**. Its stated primary objective is the development of children's self-esteem. Phone: (619) 231-1311; box office (619) 239-8355. Web site: **www.juniortheatre.com**.

Spreckels Organ

The Spreckels Organ and elegant pavilion that embraces it were gifts to the city of San Diego from John D. and Adolph B. Spreckels, sons of sugar millionaire Claus Spreckels.

The largest outdoor pipe organ in the world, it was built by the Austin Organ Company of Hartford, CT, and was **first played on New Year's Eve 1914**, during the Panama-California Exposition's inaugural festivities.

Over the years, the musical integrity of the instrument has been maintained scrupulously. A complete restoration and cleaning was finished in 1981. In 1988, three sets of brilliant solo reeds were added, and in 1990 the Spreckels Organ Society raised funds for a 32-foot contra bombarde for the pedal division. With installation of a solid state memory system in 1991, the Spreckels Organ joined the computer age. It now has the capability of storing individual program registrations for several organists simultaneously.

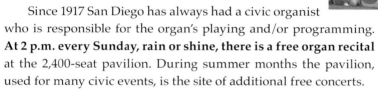

One of the world's great concert organs, the Spreckels Organ has **73 ranks, or 4,530 pipes ranging in length from 32 feet to about the size of a pencil**.

What is an organ without performance? The Spreckels Organ was played by French organist-composer Marcel Dupré in 1937 and by American virtuoso Virgil Fox in 1949.

Since 1917 San Diego has always had a civic organist who is responsible for the organ's playing and/or programming. **At 2 p.m. every Sunday, rain or shine, there is a free organ recital** at the 2,400-seat pavilion. During summer months the pavilion, used for many civic events, is the site of additional free concerts.

From mid-June through August each year, the Spreckels Organ Society presents its annual **International Summer Organ Festival**, featuring eminent theater and church organists from throughout the world on Monday evenings at 7:30 p.m.

Concert and Organ Society brochures are available at the Balboa Park Visitors Center. Phone: (619) 702-8138. Web site: **www.sosorgan.com.**

Not part of the regular programming, but...

Balboa Park is the cultural heart of a great city, and as such is host to many performing arts events produced by organizations whose primary reason for being is not necessarily performance.

Located on Park Boulevard, near Pepper Grove picnic and playground, **Centro Cultural de la Raza** and **The WorldBeat Center** are frequently performance venues for theater, dance and music.

The San Diego Museum of Art, known for its fine permanent collection and special exhibitions, also nurtures a resident chamber music ensemble, the **Westwind Brass**, which performs throughout the year in the museum's **Copley Auditorium**.

Recently, the museum instituted a series of jazz concerts held the first Wednesday of every month. Other musical events are presented from time to time.

The acclaimed **San Diego Youth Symphony** and **San Diego Civic Youth Ballet** both have their homes and rehearse in Balboa Park. Both offer important training and performance opportunities for future professional artists.

Balboa Park's facilities are alive with festivals, dance programs, and special events that fall under the general category of the performing arts. One need only inquire at the Visitors Center to be apprised of this cornucopia of cultural activity.

The community-based **Fern Street Circus** might appear, as if by magic, delighting families and children at the corner of President's Way and Park Blvd. And just about any Saturday or Sunday, one finds performers along the Prado.

Whether part of an institution or present by virtue of a day permit, the performing arts are definitely a part of the magic that is Balboa Park.

> Balboa Park's facilities are alive with festivals, dance programs, and special events that fall under the general category of the performing arts.

CHAPTER 6
RECREATIONAL OPPORTUNITIES

with contributions by Roger Conlee and Mary Anderson

Most visitors to San Diego only see and experience a fraction of the wonderful things Balboa Park has to offer. They concentrate their activities in the cultural heart of the Park and never venture east to the Morley Field recreational area, or west of Cabrillo Bridge to the Sixth Avenue area. Expand your exploration of the Park to these two corridors, and you'll expand your appreciation of San Diego's healthy outdoor lifestyle, and may just get a good work-out in the process!

British-style lawn bowling is alive and well in Balboa Park

Name your game

Whether your favorite sport is horseshoes or bocce ball;, throwing a Frisbee® or table tennis, archery, swimming or playing golf, you can find it in Balboa Park. It's all in knowing where to look and whom to call to find out when there's open play. Almost everyone is familiar with the **English-style lawn bowling courts** located near the Laurel Street entrance to the Park, but did you know that you can also play bocce (the Italian version) and petanque (the French version) in Balboa Park?

Some of the playing fields and courts are managed by private groups who schedule regular games/matches and other events for their members, but almost all offer some open play time for public use and most offer lessons. Some may charge a small fee or ask for a donation to help maintain their site. Some are open and available as long as they are not in use by the club. If you are interested in one of the activities managed by a private group, it's a good idea to call first.

There are three primary centers for recreational activity in Balboa Park:

East Mesa: area between 28th Street and Florida Canyon

Balboa Park Golf Course

A blue-collar course with million-dollar views. Situated atop the Park's East Mesa, this public course offers spectacular vistas of downtown San Diego and the bay. Sam Sneed holds the course record with a score of 60. Both Tiger Woods and Phil Mickelson won Junior World Golf Championships here. And it's the most inexpensive 18-hole course in the city you can play!

There's a **nine-hole executive course** in addition to the **par-72, 18-hole course**. Greens fees are reasonable, with generous discounts to San Diego City residents who obtain a PIN (personal identification number) for computerized reservations. Twilight and senior discounts, lessons, and rentals of carts and clubs are available. Facilities include a golf shop, driving range, putting green and coffee shop. The historic clubhouse is badly in need of renovation, but at press time, the earliest this is projected to happen is 2015.

The first five fairways, especially the fifth, are narrow and bordered by canyons. Watch out if you have a slice! A redesign of the 18-hole course in the mid-1990's was unpopular with some golfers, adding longer walks, in some cases steep climbs, from green to next tee. The setting and soft breezes off the bay make up for most of the shortcomings. The **spectacular view from the 16th hole** alone will make your day.

The course hosts the **City Amateur Tournament** in June, with men's, women's and senior's competitions; and the Union-Tribune and Phil Mickelsen junior tournaments in April and August, respectively. Golf shop: (619) 239-1660. Balboa Park Golf Course: (619) 235-1184; computerized reservations: (619) 570-1234.

Morley Field Sports Complex

Located at Texas and Upas Streets near the Park's northeast corner, this vast sports compound, named for longtime park superintendent John Morley, offers facilities for a wide range of participant sports. Driving in the main entrance, you'll be facing the **public swimming pool**. Just to your right, a large information board and map will get you oriented. Facing the complex, the **tennis courts** are to the right (west), the **ball diamonds** straight ahead beyond the pool, and the **archery and disc golf ranges** a considerable distance to the left (east). Good information on the whole complex is a click or two away on the Web site: www.morleyfield.com. The site is maintained by the Disc Golf Club, which understandably dominates the home page.

- **Archery Target Range:** Nine target backs for daytime public use. The San Diego Archery Club holds shoots, or rounds, the first and third Sundays of each month at 9 a.m. Located along Pershing Drive at the far east side of the Morley Field complex, north of the golf course. Phone: (619) 687-3373; Website: www.sandiegoarchers.com.
- **Balboa Tennis Club:** One of the area's oldest and finest tennis facilities. Twenty-five courts for singles and doubles play, which must be reserved. Club memberships are reasonably priced—even less for seniors 60 and over—and are renewable at a discount. Junior and three-month permits also available. Members may reserve courts in advance. Non-members pay a modest day fee and must sign up on-site. Lessons available. Free junior clinics Tuesdays at 4 p.m. Food, snacks and tennis gear available. Information: (619) 295-9278. Lessons: (619) 291-5248.
- The lighted **Maureen Connolly Stadium**, named for a San Diego tennis great of yesteryear, hosts tournaments, including the U.S. National 25 & Over Championships in November. The Balboa Open Tournament is held in

July, the Balboa Junior Championships in early August, and the Metro Championships in September. Biggest tournament, drawing 800 entrants: the San Diego District Championships in August. Most heart-warming: the National Wheelchair Tournament, also in August. Call the Balboa Tennis Club for tournament information (phone numbers listed above).

- **Baseball Field:** The full-size baseball diamond is San Diego City College's home field. Can be reserved. (619) 525-8262.
- **Bocce Courts:** Open free during daylight hours. First-come, first-served. Players must provide their own equipment. Far northeast corner of Morley Field complex, at Upas and Jacaranda Drive.
- **Bud Kearns Swimming Pool:** Open all year. A small fee is charged. Economical multi-use passes available. Lessons available, as are recreational swim team, youth water polo and water exercise programs. Pool can be rented for birthday, school and office parties and other special events. (619) 692-4920.
- **Disc (Frisbee®) Golf:** 18-hole course open during daylight hours. First-come, first-served. Small fee. Lessons and disc rentals available. Course closed for tournaments the first Saturday and Sunday in December, and the first Saturday in May. Located along Pershing Drive at the far east side of the Morley Field complex just north of the Archery Range. View the course on its Web site: **www.morleyfield.com**. (619) 692-3607.
- **Dog Exercise and Training Leash-Free Area:** A sloping grassy area just west of the tennis courts is set aside for dogs to run loose for exercise and training.
- **Fitness Course:** A two-mile jogging or walking trail with 18 exercise stations. Free to the public during daylight hours. Starts just across parking lot north of tennis courts and meanders throughout the Morley complex.
- **Multipurpose Athletic Fields:** Four fields for softball, youth baseball, soccer and rugby. One is lighted. Batting cage, snack bar. Home of the Pioneer Pony League and North Park Little League, whose Ted Williams Field,

honoring the San Diego-born batting king, was refurbished by the San Diego Padres. Reservations required and a fee is charged. Contact the Recreation Center Director: (619) 525-8262 or log on to **www.sandiego.gov/park-and-recreation/centers/morley.shtml**.

- **Sandieson Cottage:** French Club operates courts for petanque, which is similar to bocce or lawn bowling. East of pool, north of ball fields. (619) 281-7923.

- **Tiny Tot Play Area:** Recently upgraded with newer play equipment, this area is surrounded by grassy picnic area with tables. Located between swimming pool and ball fields.

- **Velodrome:** One of only 17 world-class bicycle tracks in the U.S. Open to the public for cycling or blading Monday, Wednesday and Saturday mornings from 9 a.m. to noon. Must have a mechanically sound bike or in-line skates. Races conducted by the Southern California Velodrome Association Tuesday nights, April through August. Kids' fun races at 6:30 p.m., the serious stuff at 7:00. Spectators pay a small donation. This lighted, 333-meter track hosted the Junior National Championships in 1998. **Many Olympic teams, including the U.S. and Brazil, have trained here**. Six-week adult development classes include bike, helmet and coaching. A fee is charged. A six-week youth training program is free. (619) 260-3701. Web site: **www.sdvelodrome.com**.

Florida Canyon Nature Trails:

Florida Canyon divides the Park's East and Central Mesas. Balboa Naval Medical Center occupies the canyon's south end, while the northern portion remains a wilderness. Marked hiking/mountain bike trails meander through rocky hillsides of sagebrush, cactus and other natural flora. Start near the dog-off-leash area behind the Morley Field tennis courts. Another trail on the canyon's west side starts at the Desert Garden just across Park Blvd. from the Bea Evenson Fountain (Plaza de Balboa). If walking, wear sturdy walking shoes. Park Rangers also lead tours. (619) 235-1122.

Also on the East Mesa, near Morley Field...

- Bird Park
- Cedar Street Children's Play Area
- Golden Hill Park
- Grape Street Park

Central Mesa: area between Florida Canyon and Cabrillo Canyon

Archery Field Range

Maintained by the San Diego Archery Club, which holds shoots and rounds on the first and third Sundays of each month at 9 a.m., at this and the Archery Target Range at Morley Field. **The Field Range is a cross-country** course that begins next to the restrooms and the parking lot at Alcazar Garden (behind the House of Charm). Ph: (619) 687-3373; Web site: **www.sandiegoarchers.com**.

Balboa Park Activity Center

A massive facility on Park Boulevard, just west of the Park Administration building, houses **excellent badminton, table tennis and volleyball courts**. The Center annually hosts large special events such as **national gymnastics and table tennis tournaments, Special Olympics, Senior Olympics, regional science fairs** and **local volleyball tournaments**. Badminton use is controlled by the Balboa Park Badminton Club. Play is free on a first-come, first-served sign-up basis. No phone reservations. Badminton is played in the afternoon on Tuesdays, Thursdays, and Saturdays and Sundays; table tennis is played in the evenings on Mondays, Tuesdays, Thursdays and Fridays and during the day on Saturdays and Sundays. A small fee is charged for table tennis. For more information on table tennis www.sdtta.org. Free open volleyball play is scheduled on Monday and Wednesday evenings. Signups on-site. To join an adult volleyball league, call (619) 584-GAME. The Activity Center can be rented: (858) 581-7100. Schedule is subject to change; call the Activity Center for a current schedule or log on to **www.sandiego.gov/park-and-recreation/parks/activctr.shtml**.

Municipal Gymnasium

The venerable "Muni Gym" has been renovated just west of the Hall of Champions in the Palisades area. This the site of a legendary one-on-one basketball match between local hero and Park-area resident Bill Walton and Kareem Abdul Jabar.

Once basketball-only, it's now **also used for volleyball, badminton, table tennis, and disabled team sports activities** such as quad(riplegic) rugby. Occasionally, square dancing, art fairs and traveling exhibits are booked. There's a fee to reserve the gym for a tournament, otherwise use is free. Information and reservations: (619) 525-8262.

Blind Community Center

Exciting programs include crafts, exercise, gourmet cooking and computer classes, choral group and a talking books library. This newer facility is located at Park Boulevard and Upas Street, across Park Boulevard from the War Memorial Building at north end of Zoo parking lot. A **small one-time fee provides lifetime membership**. 1805 Upas Street. (619) 298-5021.

Therapeutic recreation services

Numerous programs for the physically and mentally challenged include: Leisure Seekers (mentally ill or emotionally disabled); Action Seekers (developmentally disabled); Independent Club (learning-impaired or brain-injured who can use public transit); Let's Get Physical (MS, cerebral palsy or spinal cord-injured); Adventurers (brain-injured, hearing or visual impairments); Recovery (drug or alcohol abuse recoverers). Free or small-fee classes in creative writing, arts, crafts, games. Campouts, bowling and biking programs are also available. War Memorial Building at north end of Zoo parking lot. (619) 525-8247. Hearing impaired: (619) 525-8249.

Dance classes

Everything from hip hop to jazz ballet, from folk dancing to ballroom dancing is available in Balboa Park. Walk in and pay a small fee for beginning classes in waltz, cha-cha, fox trot or swing on Fridays and Sundays; or participate in intermediate and advanced levels of international folk dances for a mere $1.00

donation on Mondays. If you prefer to just watch, international folk dancing is featured every Sunday in the Balboa Park Club from 12:30 - 5:00 p.m. for dancers and spectators.

Thirteen different dance clubs are sponsored by the San Diego Park and Recreation Department in an organization called the **International Dance Association of San Diego County**. Most of these classes take place at the Balboa Park Club or the Recital Hall, both located in the Palisades area. For more info, call (619) 422-1584, pick up a yellow brochure at the Visitors Center, or access their Web site: **http://idasdc.org**. For a Web site with photos and links to the different clubs, try: **www.balboapark.org** and search "Dance."

If you prefer a regular semester-long program, those 15 and over can participate in **traditional ballet, tap, musical theatre dance, jazz, hip hop, and Hawaiian dance training** for a small fee per semester. Most of these weekly classes are scheduled at the Casa del Prado on the second floor, or in the War Memorial Building near the San Diego Zoo. All levels are available. Special programs are available for children (although these may take place at other recreation center locations besides Balboa Park), and some are geared for seniors. Recitals take place in June each year.

Advanced students may audition for membership in the San Diego Civic Dance Company, which performs several times each year, including an annual dance festival in February at the Casa del Prado Theater. Serious young ballet students may become members of the **San Diego Civic Youth Ballet**, which has been offering high-quality ballet instruction at an affordable price since 1944. Call (619) 233-3060. For more information on all San Diego Park and Recreation Department dance classes, call (619) 525-8258 or (619) 235-5255.

Balboa Park Senior Lounge

Located in the Casa del Prado building, the Senior Lounge is now open seven days a week from 10 a.m. to 4 p.m., and is manned by a great group of volunteers. Look for a sandwich board out front of the building on El Prado near the Lily Pond. The Lounge offers a place to relax and talk to local residents over a cup of coffee, or play board and card games. Free regularly scheduled guided walks, book discussions, jazz listening and art classes are also offered.

One wheelchair is available for check-out. To reserve the chair, call the lounge between 10 a.m. and 4 p.m., at (619) 236-0262.

Also in the Central Mesa recreational area...
- Accredited 10K course
- Balboa Park Visitors Center for information on walking tours—both cultural and recreational
- Florida Canyon hiking/mountain biking trails
- Palm Canyon short hiking trail
- Gold Gulch hiking trail
- Marston Addition hiking trail
- Pepper Grove Children's Discovery Playground
- San Diego Zoo with 5 miles of walking trails

West Mesa: area between Sixth Avenue and Cabrillo Canyon

San Diego Lawn Bowling Club

An old British Commonwealth pastime flourishes at the San Diego Lawn Bowling Club in the Sixth Avenue area on the Park's west side. The club is for members only, but you're welcome to watch, take a free lesson, and inquire about joining.

You can see the bowlers every day at 1 p.m. just west of Cabrillo Bridge and north of Laurel Street, and on Tuesday and Thursday mornings from spectator benches alongside the wide green courts. Tournaments pitting San Diego's lawn bowlers against clubs from other cities are often held on weekends.

If you take your free lesson and are still interested, three to four additional lessons can be taken for $12. Then, if you and the club are still simpatico, a one-year membership costs $110.

Lawn bowling began in Great Britain and spread to Canada, Australia, India and the American Colonies. For more information, call (619) 238-5457 or log on to **www. sandiegolawnbowling.com**.

Redwood (Bridge) Club

The Redwood Club hosts bridge games every day (except Sunday) at 12:30 p.m. There is a small annual club membership fee. Non-members may play for $1 a game. Duplicate bridge is played but no points are given. Near Sixth Avenue and Redwood Street in the former roque and shuffleboard clubhouse, next to the children's playground. Shuffleboard and roque courts still exist but are not in good playable condition. Phone: (619) 291-5625.

Balboa Club

The Balboa Club is home of the **San Diego Chess Club** and the **San Diego Horseshoe Club**. Open daily from noon to 6 p.m., at Sixth Avenue and Ivy Street in the Park's southwest corner. There's a small annual membership fee for the chess club. Non-members may play for $1 a day. Kids learn in summertime weeklong **Children's Chess Camp** sessions. U.S. Chess Federation games are played Wednesdays at 7 p.m. San Diego Chess Championships take place January through April. (619) 239-7166.

To play horseshoes, bring your own equipment. These are the **only pits in San Diego County sanctioned by the National Horseshoe Pitching Association**. Members participate in six national tournaments annually. Low annual membership fee. For information on tournaments and/or membership in the the San Diego Horseshoe Club, call (619) 238-9352.

Also on the West Mesa, near Sixth Avenue...
- Dog off-leash area
- In-line skating and biking along Balboa Drive
- Level, open areas often used for soccer, croquet, and volleyball games
- Old Bridle Trail for hiking and mountain biking
- Sixth Avenue Children's Play Area
- Self-guided tree walks (use free guide from Visitors Center and start at Kate Session's statue)

CHAPTER 7
HORTICULTURAL FEATURES

by Mary Anderson

While Balboa Park most often calls to mind museums and the world famous San Diego Zoo, the Park is also well known for its horticulture. With nearly 1,200 acres of parkland remaining today, Balboa Park is one of the largest and most lushly planted urban parks in the United States. Within its boundaries are a variety of beautiful gardens maintained by the San Diego Park and Recreation Department.

Moreton Bay Fig planted prior to 1915 Expo

When the city fathers dedicated City Park in 1868, the area was an arid, rocky expanse of chaparral and scrub. That began changing in 1892, when Kate Sessions leased 32 of the original 1,400 acres for a nursery and botanical garden. At the same time the city fathers named Kate Sessions "City Gardener" in order to avoid any legal problems that might have arisen had they leased parkland for commercial purposes to a private individual. No one would object to the City Gardener improving city land.

In return for the lease, Kate Sessions pledged to plant 100 trees every year for 10 years in the Park, and also to donate 300 trees and other plants to be placed elsewhere in the city. She carried out her end of the bargain faithfully, planting exotic trees and shrubs for years, thus becoming known as the "Mother of Balboa Park."

A statue in her honor, created by native San Diegan Ruth Hayward, was dedicated April 1, 1998, and is located at the west end of the Cabrillo Bridge on the southwest corner of Sefton Plaza. A self-guided walk of the West Mesa, covering its history and horticulture, is available with the starting point at the statue. (Ask for a free brochure outlining the walk at the Balboa Park Visitors Center.)

On the east side of Balboa Park, **Florida Canyon represents the Park as it was in the early 1900s.** With the exception of Florida Street bisecting the canyon, it is a peaceful, unimproved portion of Balboa Park. The native plants remain and a nature trail has been built, used by hundreds of students and other groups who want to see native San Diego plant and animal life.

> Today there are about 16,000 trees growing in Balboa Park, including over 400 different species.

Today **there are nearly 16,000 trees growing in Balboa Park**, including over **400 different species**. Although eucalyptus appears to be the predominant tree in the overall landscape, actually only 35% of the trees are eucalyptus species. These are some of the oldest and tallest trees in Balboa Park, but other towering species still growing on the West Mesa where Kate Sessions had her nursery, include several species of pines and araucaria.

Over the past 140 years, Balboa Park has grown from chaparral and scrub to a lush, and very popular, visitor destination. The gardens of Balboa Park have matured and now stand on their own as a visitor attraction. A knowledgeable Park and Recreation grounds maintenance staff, with the advice of a city horticulturist, work to preserve and protect these treasures. Under their able care, and the protection of hundreds of dedicated plant-loving volunteers and Park advocates, they will continue to flourish and attract visitors for years to come.

Gardens and other botanical features

While the entire park is a bonanza of plantings, flowerings, and foliage, formal garden areas abound in Balboa Park. Unless otherwise noted, these are open year-round and are free:

Alcazar Garden

Located adjacent to the House of Charm. It was recently renovated to replicate a 1935 design by San Diego architect Richard Requa, patterned after the gardens of Alcazar Castle in Seville, Spain. This formal garden is planted with 7,000 annuals for a year-round display of color.

Activity Center Garden Court

A formal garden courtyard between the modern Activity Center and the old Naval Hospital's historic landmark building has been effectively landscaped and developed to blend the old and the new. Today the lovely, old pink building with the twin towers, functions as the Balboa Park Administration Center. All around it are formally landscaped walkways, benches and fountains. Some have been historically reconstructed. This area of the Park is appropriately known as Inspiration Point.

Botanical Building

Located on the Prado, just east of the Museum of Art. It was the largest wood lath structure in the world when it was built in 1915 for the Panama-California Exposition. The building is 250 feet long, by 75 feet wide and 60 feet tall. It **contains about 2,100 permanent tropical plants as well as seasonal plantings**. (Open daily except Thursdays and city holidays from 10 a.m. to 4 p.m. Free). The Lily Pond is just south of the Botanical Building. The main pond and a smaller companion pool contain water lilies and lotus, which bloom from spring to fall.

Old Cactus Garden

Located on the west side of the Balboa Park Club. It was developed for the 1935 California Pacific International Exposition and contains some of the largest cactus and succulent specimens in the Park. There are also some exotic African and Australian Protea plants.

Desert Garden

Located north of the footbridge that crosses Park Boulevard near the Natural History Museum. Encompassing 2.5 acres, there are some 1,300 plants, including succulents and drought-resistant plants from around the world. Peak blooming period occurs from January to March.

FDR Grove

Located just east of the intersection of Sixth Avenue and Quince Drive. In 1995, in recognition of the 50th anniversary of the death of Franklin Delano Roosevelt, cities throughout the nation planted trees in commemoration of his leadership in protecting our country's environment. The California Conservation Corps participated in the planting of 100 Monterey cypress trees that were later killed by a fungus. These have been replaced by several species of tall araucaria trees—native to Australia and New Zealand—and there are plans to add conifers from other parts of the world in the near future. A redwood sign marks the location of the grove for visitors.

Casa del Rey Moro Gardens

The terraced garden behind the House of Hospitality was restored at the same time the building underwent reconstruction, which was completed in 1997. One of San Diego's most popular wedding sites, the open-space garden features a wishing well, small pond, ficus trees and African tulip trees, among other trees and plants. An explanation of the restoration including photographs of the formal gardens in Ronda, Spain, on which they were modeled, can be found on a rock wall just east of main terrace area of the gardens

Japanese Friendship Garden

Located northeast of the Spreckels Organ Pavilion. The garden is a place of contemplation for visitors, with **Japanese garden concepts and symbolism adapted to the climate and topography of San Diego**. The garden was recently renovated and expanded. New features include an entry plaza, tea stand, koi pond, activity center, wisteria arbor, and strolling paths. The garden's entrance plaza and adjoining observation deck are open 24 hours and are free. Garden area is open daily except Monday from 10 a.m. to 4 p.m. There is a small fee. Docent tours are available. Public information (619) 232-2780 Web site: **www.niwa.org**.

Marston House Garden

Located on the grounds of the Marston House (historical museum) at 3525 Seventh Avenue. Nationally known landscape architects George Cook, John Nolen, Thomas Church, and Hal Walker designed the original landscaping. Kate Sessions was the "horticultural consultant" when the first trees were planted in 1906. The formal garden was designed by Hal Walker and William Templeton Johnson in 1927 and installed for the 50th wedding anniversary of Park supporters George and Anna Gunn Marston. Today the flower beds brim with colorful annuals and roses.

Moreton Bay Fig Tree

Located north of the Natural History Museum. This tree was planted for the 1915 Exposition, and now nearly 100 years old, stands over 60 feet tall with a spread of 120 feet. Generations of children have climbed over its gnarled roots and into its branches. While climbing on this prize specimen is now prohibited, the area around it remains a popular picnic area for Park visitors. Other Moreton Bay fig trees are interspersed throughout the Park, but this one is the best known and has become a landmark.

> **Hint:** Golden Hill Park, near the Balboa Park Golf Course, has two of these climbable Moreton Bay fig trees that are still accessible to children. There is another one on the west side of the Park near the statue of Kate Sessions at Sixth Avenue and Laurel Street.

Palm Canyon

Located south of the House of Charm. It covers two acres and contains 450 palms of over 75 species. The original Mexican fan palms, which are most prominent, date back to the early 1900s, when an underground stream was discovered in this area. Stone steps on each side of the middle of the canyon used to lead to a wooden bridge from which brides and grooms would traditionally toss a coin and make a wish on their wedding day.

Rose Garden (Inez Grant Parker Memorial Rose Garden)

Located south of the footbridge that crosses Park Blvd. near the Natural History Museum. An All-American Rose Selection Display Garden, which **contains over over 1,750 rose bushes in 125 varieties**. This garden was also recently named one of the top 16 rose gardens in the world by the World Rose Society. The society bases its choices for the award on exceptional gardens from a historical, educational and/or visual point of view.

While many roses are in bloom from March to December, the **peak bloom is seen in April and May**. Consequently this area is one of the most popular wedding spots in the Park.

Trees for Health

The Trees for Health Garden is an arboretum of trees used for both traditional and current medical practice. The ideas is to promote a better understanding and appreciation of the value and uses of medicinal plants found around the world. Most of the trees in this medicinal garden are located on the west side of the Park, just north of Quince St. There are three more located in Redwood Circle, south of Quince, just north of the Lawn Bowling courts.

Veterans Memorial Garden

A recent addition, the Balboa Park Veterans Memorial Garden is situated on a one-acre parcel of land with three individual gardens honoring veterans--Air, Land and Sea--united by pathways leading to the Veteran's Circle, a central gathering place. Phase 1 has been completed, consisting of the Veterans Circle amphitheater and terrazzo paving encompassing quotes from Presidents Washington, Lincoln and Coolidge, relating to the principles of Honor, Duty and Country. It's located in front of the Veterans Museum and Memorial Center at 2125 Park Boulevard.

A bronze statue of a B-24 Liberator--one-sixth scale replica with an 18' wingspan--is the centerpiece of the Air Garden, soaring over a reflecting pool. Rows of red and white border roses, accented by cobalt blue agapanthus, provide a patriotic splash of color to the garden. A poppy garden with Flanders poppies is also featured.

Zoo Botanical Collection

While it is the animal collection that gets most of the attention at the Zoo, the plant collection is also impressive. The San Diego Zoo maintains an officially registered botanical garden collection, with more than 1,400 plant species. According to Zoo officials, included among those are 227 species of palms, 96 species of aloes, and **more than 700 species of orchids**, as well as 53 kinds of bamboo, 88 species of cycads, and 34 species of ginger!

> ...many of the specimens are a source of food for some of the animals.

Not only does the plant collection provide beautiful and scenic landscaping to the Zoo, many of the specimens are a source of food for some of the animals. From bamboo for the giant pandas, to eucalyptus for the koalas, and acacias for the giraffes, the plants are an important element in the animals' well being, and provide foliage for a more natural habitat. Zoo hours vary. There is a fee. Web site: **www. sandiegozoo.org**

Zoro Garden

Located between the Reuben H. Fleet Science Center and the Casa de Balboa. This is a sunken garden with a stone grotto, which was **home to a nudist colony during the 1935 Exposition**. When older, large trees were felled by a storm in the early 1990s, the once-shaded garden became a sunny environment. To accommodate the new climate, **a butterfly garden was planted containing plants that provide food for both butterfly larvae (caterpillars) and the adults**. Other plants provide nectar for the adults. Miniature indentations found in rocks collect small pools of water for the monarch, sulfur, and swallowtail butterflies that can be seen among the colorful perennials and large ficus trees that surround the garden.

Rare Kauri Tree

Of the Park's more than 15,000 trees, **one of the rarest is a New Zealand Kauri**. Planted in 1915, it is now, at over 60 feet, one of the largest kauris in California. When construction on the nearby House of Charm building threatened the tree in the early 1990s, architects redesigned a walkway in order to preserve the kauri's root system. You can find this tree just south of the walkway, which is perpendicular to the House of Charm, leading towards the statue of El Cid. It's one of the tallest trees in that area.

For more info on Balboa Park's horticulture...

The results of a Balboa Park tree survey completed by former Balboa Park Horticulturists Kathy Puplava and Paul Sirois (now district manager) have been published in a full-color spiral bound book available at the Visitors Center and the San Diego Natural History Museum.

The members of the **San Diego Botanical Garden Foundation** and the **San Diego Floral Association** hold free flower and plant shows year-round in the Casa del Prado building. Exhibits range from bonsai and bromeliads to ferns and orchids. Informative talks by local experts on the various species are offered, while plants and cuttings are available for sale. These popular shows take place on Saturdays and Sundays, usually in Room 101 at the Casa del Prado. **A year-round plant show schedule** is available through the San Diego Floral Association office, Casa del Prado, Room 105, weekdays 10 a.m. to 3 p.m., (619) 232-5762. **www.sdfloral.org** **A horticultural reference library** featuring over 4,000 volumes, is open to the public during the same hours. Current show info is available at the Balboa Park Visitors Center, (619) 239-0512.

If you are especially interested in the botanical aspects of Balboa Park, ask a volunteer at the Visitors Center for two special brochures produced by Park and Recreation Department staff. One shows you how to find all the gardens in the cultural zone and describes each one; the other offers a self-guided tree walk west of the Cabrillo Bridge, where Kate Sessions planted many exotic trees, some still growing today.

Of Special Interest

CHAPTER 8
FAIRY-TALE ARCHITECTURE

by Roger Conlee

There are several architectural styles to feast your eyes upon in Balboa Park, but **Spanish Colonial Revival** is the predominant theme, along with Mission Revival.

Spanish Colonial (also known as **Spanish Baroque**) is based on the elaborate stone architecture of Spain and Portugal, while **Mission Revival** reflects the basic adobe architecture actually practiced in early California.

House of Hospitality on Plaza de Panama

The Spanish Colonial Revival style seen in Balboa Park represents an architectural movement that began to flourish on the U.S. Pacific Coast in the 1890s. Heavily influenced by the Spanish-Moorish architecture of the Iberian Peninsula and Spanish colonial sites elsewhere, it remained popular the first three decades of the 20th century.

One of San Diego's earliest buildings of this style outside of Balboa Park, designed to serve anticipated crowds arriving for the 1915 Exposition, is the Santa Fe Depot downtown, still in use today.

The architecture that never was

It was a romanticized look at what architects and builders of the time imagined California could have been like in the early days of the European explorers and missionaries. In the words of Art Historian Will Chandler, "They fabricated a more romantic Spanish colonial history than ever existed in North America. They tried to give the appearance of 300-year-old buildings in places like

Southern California, Texas and Florida that had been occupied by Europeans for only 150 years." Elaborate trappings such as columns, finials, cornices, and intricate friezes above arched doorways exemplify Spanish Colonial. Mexican critics of the style call it "Hollywood Spanish." Balboa Park abounds in examples of this style of architecture. **The elaborate entrance to the Museum of Man emulates an ornate church outside of Mexico City, while the Museum of Art's facade is based on a building at the University of Salamanca in Spain.**

Mission Revival, on the other hand, reflects the more rudimentary construction that actually took place in Alta and Baja California, as well as Mexico's Puebla district, in the 18th and early 19th centuries.

Contrasting styles on display

Balboa Park's central quad, Plaza de Panama, presents a fine illustration of the two styles. **The elegant House of Hospitality, one of the Park's best examples of Spanish Colonial architecture**, occupies the plaza's southeast corner. Facing it on the southwest side is the **Mission Revival House of Charm. The House of Hospitality features elaborate ornamentation while the House of Charm, patterned after the Basilica de Guadalupe in Guadalajara, is an accurate depiction of the Puebla style.** The two buildings are like a lady adorned in an elegant ball gown glittering with gold and diamond accessories, alongside an equally beautiful woman in a basic dress and a single strand of pearls.

Other architectural styles you'll see in the Park include the **International Modernist**, exemplified by the Air and Space Museum at the south end of the Palisades; **Native American Pueblo**, signified by the Balboa Park Club; **Postwar Modernist**, epitomized by Frank L. Hope's Timken Museum on the northeast side of Plaza de Panama; and the Asian modes in the Japanese Friendship Garden.

> **NOTE:** *Throughout the following section, references are made to many of the most prominent buildings located in the cultural zone of Balboa Park. Although most of these structures have had various uses and names over the years, the names used here are those currently associated with the buildings.*

The first Expo: design impetus

The Park as you see it today began to take shape with planning for the **1915-16 Panama-California Exposition**. Landscape designer John C. Olmsted of Massachusetts planned simple, natural grounds for the fair, and architects **Bertram G. Goodhue** of New York and Irving Gill of San Diego were hired to complement the scheme with simple, mission-style buildings. Goodhue wanted more emphasis on architecture, however, and insisted on Spanish Colonial designs with Persian-Islamic features. Goodhue got his way. Olmsted and Gill quit.

> The Park as you see it today began to take shape with planning for the 1915-16 Panama-California Exposition.

With Goodhue seldom leaving New York, most of the expo's buildings were actually designed by his assistant, architect **Carleton Monroe Winslow**, and expo director of works **Frank P. Allen, Jr.** The Goodhue team's greatest triumph was the **Cabrillo Bridge-California Building-California Tower** complex, which still welcomes visitors at the Park's west entrance. Art Historian Chandler calls the complex "one of the most splendid adaptations of a physical site anywhere in America."

The 200-foot majestic **California Tower**, then and now the Park's signature structure, looms over the gracefully arched bridge spanning the deep Cabrillo Canyon. Inspired by a bridge in Toledo, Spain, the bridge projects a rugged yet graceful beauty from any angle, whether you view it up close, from below, or from a distant hillside. The adjacent tower, influenced by the towers of several different Spanish and Mexican churches, juts above the California Building, which today houses the **Museum of Man**. The three are all of one piece, a unified architectural concept.

The intricately tiled dome atop the Museum of Man exemplifies the Moorish influence in Spanish architecture. Inside you can still admire the Mayan pillars and murals from the 1915 Science of Man exhibit, recently restored. The facade was sculpted by the Piccirilli brothers of New York, who also worked on the Lincoln Memorial in Washington, D.C.

Survivors of the first Exposition

In addition to the California Tower/Cabrillo Bridge complex, several buildings remain today from the 1915-16 Exposition. The principal ones are the **Botanical Building** and its highly photographed reflecting pool, the **Spreckels Organ Pavilion**, and the **Balboa Park Club**. Other buildings have been rebuilt to replicate their 1935-36 appearance.

Carleton Monroe Winslow used Spanish and Persian models in designing the 75-foot-high Botanical Building. To some, the

redwood-lath dome hovering over a 250-foot long flower garden resembles a European train station.

Today's **House of Charm** on Plaza de Panama, designed by Winslow, originally was the Indian Arts Building. Native American arts and crafts were displayed there in 1915, but the building was renamed the Russia and Brazil Building for the expo's second year.

The Organ Pavilion was designed by Harrison Albright as a grand peristyle complementing a vaulted organ housing. The half-circle of Corinthian columns originally was mirrored by similar columns, now long gone, south of the House of Hospitality. The organ pavilion was donated by brothers John and Adolph Spreckels, who owned two newspapers, the city's streetcar company, and the Hotel del Coronado.

The Native American Pueblo style of the **Balboa Park Club** (originally the New Mexico Building, then the Palace of Education) was designed by the Rapp brothers of Santa Fe, New Mexico, in the style of a 16th century mission church with pueblo influences.

Saving the heritage

After the fair closed, America entered World War I and the military occupied the Park's buildings. Several years later, devoted citizens rallied to save many of them from destruction.

With roofs leaking and walls crumbling after a hard winter in 1932-33, a committee led by Gertrude Gilbert raised money at the grassroots to ward off the city's demolition plans. Despite the Great Depression, San Diegans gave dimes and dollars, and schoolchildren donated their meager allowances.

Some buildings were so far gone they couldn't be saved, but materials salvaged from those were used to renovate the others. **Richard S. Requa**, who later emerged as one of the foremost architects in Park history, oversaw the operation. Most of the buildings had skylights at that time, and Requa salvaged enough glass from the doomed buildings to replace all the skylights in those being renovated.

Meanwhile, two significant new buildings enhanced El Prado's landscape. William Templeton Johnson designed both the **Museum of Art** (1926) and the **Natural History Museum** (1933). The façade of the first reflected a style of ornamentation fashionable during the early Spanish Renaissance, while the second incorporated a monumental Italianate style.

The Requa era

Enthused by the success of Chicago's 1933-34 World's Fair, San Diego planned another major fair for 1935-36, the **California Pacific International Exposition**.

Requa, the Exposition's official architect, and his associates designed more than eighty percent of the fair's new structures. These included **Spanish Village**, fifteen **House of Pacific Relations** cottages, and the redesign of the House of Hospitality and adjacent gardens. He also redesigned the first Expo's Montezuma Garden into today's charming **Alcazar Garden**, patterned after the gardens at the Alcazar in Seville, Spain.

Requa's masterpiece is the **House of Hospitality**. Its exterior exhibits classic Spanish Colonial features from the 1915 Expo, studded with elaborate accessories that include ornate doorways and rows of classical ornamental motifs on the frieze above the windows. Ceiling beams in the Alhambra meeting room are based on those in the Monastery of Santo Domingo de Silos in Spain.

The inner courtyard, surrounded by typical Mediterranean-style arcades, is set off by **Donal Hord**'s oft-photographed sculpture of the "**Woman of Tehuantepec**." The Spanish-Moorish garden to the south, a popular site for weddings, is patterned on the garden at a palace in Ronda, Spain.

The International Modernist **Ford Building** was built in an incredible 88 days. Commissioned by the Detroit automaker and designed by Walter D. Teague, it reflected the latest in design and technology at the time, and resembles similar facilities built by automakers for other world's fairs in the '30s. A few steps away, the Ford (now Starlight) Bowl was designed by Vern D. Knudson, an acoustics expert, for symphonic and other musical performances at the expo.

Echoes of the second Expo

Today's Park visitor can admire many buildings that survive from the 1935-36 Exposition. In addition to the House of Hospitality and House of Charm on Plaza de Panama, don't miss **Spanish Village** located behind the Natural History Museum. The **International Cottages of the House of Pacific Relations** can be seen near the Organ Pavilion. In the Palisades area (Pan American Plaza), examples include: the **Recital Hall** with its **Marie Hitchcock Puppet Theater** (formerly The Women's Palace); **Air & Space Museum** (Ford Building); **Automotive Museum** (1935 California State Building); **Municipal Gymnasium** (Palace of Electricity and Varied Industries); **San Diego Hall of Champions** (Federal Building) and **Starlight Bowl** (Ford Bowl).

New additions, replicated oldies

The Postwar Modern **Timken Museum**, designed by Frank L. Hope, is clad in marble imported from Italy, trimmed in bronze. The gallery opened in 1965, a major and controversial departure from the Park's Spanish Colonial influence.

Architect Louis Bodmer, formerly assistant to William Templeton Johnson, designed the **Reuben H. Fleet Space Theater and Science Center**, which opened in 1973, in Spanish Colonial style (now known as simply the Reuben H. Fleet Science Center).

The Japanese Friendship Garden opened in 1990, featuring indigenous Japanese architecture and landscaping.

Historic replication has been the byword in postwar Balboa Park. The most significant reconstructions undertaken by the City of San Diego have been the **Casa del Prado, Casa de Balboa, House of Charm** and **House of Hospitality**. The former Palace of Food & Beverages from 1935-36 was rebuilt as Casa del Prado. Reopened in 1971, it houses many meeting rooms, dance studios and rehearsal space supporting the adjacent Casa del Prado Theater. Just opposite that complex, construction of the Casa de Balboa in the early 1980s was necessitated by a fire that destroyed the original building.

The Houses of Charm and Hospitality were razed and reconstructed in the mid-1990s. The House of Hospitality re-emerged in an historically accurate depiction of its 1935-36 remodel, winning prestigious awards. Much ornamentation was saved and replaced on the building; others were authentically reproduced. Milford Wayne Donaldson was the architect, Will Chandler the project historian. In the late 1990s, Architect Richard Bundy designed an extensive remodel, addition and stunning new entrance on the north side of the San Diego Natural History Museum, which was opened in 2000.

Fountains and faces

The Park has had many lovely fountains over the years. Gone but fondly remembered is the Firestone Singing Fountain in front of the Ford Building, where colored jets of light splashed through dancing waters. Built for the 1935-36 Expo, it was a casualty of World War II.

Today's most prominent water feature is the 1972 **Bea Evenson Fountain**, shooting jets of water 50 to 60 feet high at the east end of El Prado. On a summer day, its wide, circular concrete base can be crowded with visitors removing their shoes and socks, cooling their feet and keeping an eye on their wading youngsters. **The well fountain in Spanish Village was built for the 1935 Expo.** Two large punchbowl fountains flank the facade of the Botanical Building. Designed for the 1915 Expo, they were remodeled in 1960, with blue mosaic glass tiles lining their basins, and more recently received new sculpted finials. Original drawings were recovered from the basement of the San Diego Central Library to recreate the whimsical fountains from the 1915 Panama-California Exposition.

The handsome new **Plaza de Panama Fountain** was a gift in 1996 from Mary Elizabeth North, in memory of her parents. Water pours from a vessel in the hands of Donal Hord's "**Woman of Tehuantepec**" in the House of Hospitality's patio fountain. In the garden to the south are a series of Moorish, low-basin fountains designed by Requa.

> Tucked away at the end of a pathway between the Casa de Balboa and the House of Hospitality, is the Persian Water Carpet.

Tucked away at the end of a pathway between the Casa de Balboa and the House of Hospitality, is the **Persian Water Carpet**. A Requa-designed fountain, it has been restored to its original splendor. Behind the House of Charm, **two ornate Moorish fountains of yellow, green and blue tile in Alcazar Garden were also designed by Requa and date from 1935.**

A bearded face spews water into the fountain on the east side of the Museum of Man. Look closely and you'll see other interesting stone and concrete faces staring at you from the Park's walls, niches and fountains, especially along El Prado between the Panama and Balboa Plazas.

Small faces decorate the tops of columns fronting the Casa de Balboa on the south side of El Prado. Have your camera ready and look for faces also peering from the ornamentation on Casa del Prado. More statues and faces stare down from the Museum of Art's ornate facade. Take a moment to admire the noble Mayan face on the previously noted House of Hospitality fountain.

In the Plaza de Panama look closely at the statue of **El Cid**, not only at the determined face of the Spanish hero, but that of his proud steed. At the west end of El Prado, **statues of seven historical figures occupy niches on the breathtaking facade of the Museum of Man** (California Building). These include the explorer Cabrillo and Father Serra, the California missions' founder. These were sculpted by the Picirilli brothers, who also worked on the Lincoln Memorial in Washington, D.C. Various faces and agony masks also adorn the tops of the columns at the Spreckels Organ Pavilion.

The newest statues to appear in Balboa Park are on the west side, near Sixth Avenue and Laurel Street. Here you will find a charming rendition of Kate Sessions, famed Park horticulturist called the "Mother of Balboa Park," on one side of Laurel, while across the street three historic male figures reside. Standing are Alonzo Horton and Ephraim Morse, two of the original Park founders in 1868, while seated close by is George Marston, important civic leader, early Park advocate and donor whose original home in Balboa Park, just a few blocks north of his statue, is now a museum. Ruth Hayward sculpted all four statues.

The best in four corners

The architecture is fascinating throughout Balboa Park. Here are some of the best features to admire in four corners of the Park's popular cultural core:

- **South**—The **San Diego Air and Space Museum** is the best preserved of the old buildings in the south Palisades area and a **fine example of the International Modernist trend of the 1920s and '30s.** Nearby buildings were once elaborately decorated, but have lost much of their ornamentation over the years, with the exception of the recently restored facade of the Federal Building (now housing the San Diego Hall of Champions Sports Museum).
- **West**—**California Tower and Building**, grandly Spanish Colonial. The tower is one of San Diego's principal landmarks.
- **Central**—**House of Hospitality**, its stately elegance dominating the southeast corner of Plaza de Panama.
- **North**—**The Casa del Prado Building (and Theater)** puts a Spanish Colonial glow on the northeast face of El Prado.

> **Hint:** Free tours of the Spanish Colonial architecture along El Prado, are offered by the Committee of 100 on the first Wednesday of every month at 9:30 a.m. Tour begins at the Balboa Park Visitors Center. For more information, call: (619) 223-6566.

CHAPTER 9
BALBOA PARK FOR FAMILIES

by Susan Bernstein

Families can plan educational experiences, fun-packed play, or enjoyable entertainment in Balboa Park. The Park has something for all interests and ages. Are you interested in art, science, Air and Space, anthropology or natural history? Would your children like to watch a puppet show, ride a train, or play on a jungle gym? Or, would they rather learn how to tumble gems, paint a ceramic pot, or identify ancient fossils?

Taking a ride on the 1910 Carousel

It's easy to plan visits to museums with a theme in mind. For example, a day spent learning about transportation would include visits to the San Diego Model Railroad Museum, Automotive and Air and Space Museums, with picnics and play time in the Organ Pavilion near the Lily Pond. You could end with a ride on the Miniature Train near the San Diego Zoo.

I have fond memories of taking my son, Ben, to many performances at the Puppet Theater. Our Friday morning routine included seeing the show, having a picnic lunch near the House of Pacific Relations (International Cottages), and playing in the Park before his afternoon nap. One very special day, we saw a puppetry troupe that performed in San Diego as part of a Soviet Arts Festival. The variety of puppets we enjoyed inspired me to try my own hand, and I now have a collection of animal puppets and animal hot pads that double as puppets in a pinch.

Other memorable times were those spent just watching entertainers along Balboa Park's main thoroughfares. My family and I have enjoyed impromptu concerts on a Balinese gamelan and ancient Mexican instruments, or watched clowns and magicians. Strolling in the Park today, you might see paper flower making, jugglers, or palm readers. Bring your lunch and settle into a wonderful and entertaining afternoon.

When the children's attention wanes, explore Zoro Gardens, just west of the Reuben H. Fleet Science Center. The beds are planted with summertime wildflowers, attracting multitudes of butterflies. Or guide them through the cool, shady Botanical Building with its mossy waterfalls and raised "scent garden" at the west end of the building.

Almost all the museums, theaters, and the Zoo provide summer and weekend classes for children. Check their Web sites, or call the individual organizations' education departments for more details.

Here are some suggested activities for families with young children (pre-schoolers and early grades), and for children 8 or older. Most of these "children's outings" are as fun for adults as they are for children. Suggestions aren't listed in any particular order. Please refer to the enclosed map and map codes for the exact locations.

Special activities for younger children (Pre-school through 2nd grade)

"Kid City," Reuben H. Fleet Science Center

"Kid City" is a hands-on activity center for children up to age six. From conveyer belts and cranes to air chutes and grocery stores, young visitors will work, create, play, and learn as they experience the wonders of the every day working world within this exhibition. Tips and strategies are offered on parent-child interaction to encourage children's learning. "Kid City" is one of the only spaces in any of the museums in Balboa Park designed for the very young.

Many of the other exhibits in the Science Center are also suitable for young children. The displays encourage exploration and discovery and most everything is "touchable. Visitors move from one display to another, following their own agenda. Experiential learning is the basic tenet of this institution.

Balboa Park Puppet Guild

The Puppet Guild has been entertaining youngsters since 1947, with matinee performances in the Marie Hitchcock Puppet Theater in Balboa Park. On Wednesdays through Fridays puppet shows are performed twice each day, with added shows on Saturdays, Sundays and holidays. Weekday shows are also added during the summer months. Tickets may be purchased in advance or at the door. It is advisable to call for specific information about the show and to verify performance times.

The puppeteers are professionals and volunteers, and their shows appeal to young children. They perform traditional and contemporary stories with individually crafted puppets. A variety of marionettes, hand, rod and shadow puppets are used. Each show is different; the style of puppetry depends on the individual puppeteer.

Botanical Building

Don't overlook this huge open lath structure as a place to take children. Not only does it have a wonderful, jungle feel, but there are two areas that will be of special interest to them. Near the entrance is a raised bed with herbs of all varieties, where visitors are encouraged to touch and sniff. The best way to do so, is to rub the leaves of the plant between your fingers and then to raise your fingers to your nostrils to smell. Kids love this. However, make sure they don't do this to every plant in the building—only the herb section is designed for this type of activity!

Nearby is a bed of carnivorous plants in a boggy landscape. The older children in your group will especially enjoy seeing Venus Fly Traps and Pitcher Plants up close (these plants capture the nutrients they need by ingesting insects).

Carousel and Miniature Train

The classic 1910 Balboa Park Carousel is easy to find—just follow the calliope music when you arrive in the vicinity of the

huge Moreton Bay Fig tree behind the Natural History Museum. The Carousel lies just north and east of Spanish Village, close to Park Blvd. The Miniature Train ride leaves its station nearby.

These two rides are highlighted by the Carousel, a 1910 structure, open daily in winters on Saturdays, Sundays, and holidays, 11 a.m.-5:30 p.m. (4:30 for the Miniature Train ride), and daily during the summer and school holiday periods. The cost is $1.50 per ticket per person, while children under one year old ride for free. Tickets can be purchased at a booth nearby. On the Carousel, young children have the choice of riding on a horse, zebra, or sitting on a decorated bench, while older children grab for the brass ring. If one is snagged, they get a free ride. The Balboa Park Carousel is one of only a dozen in the United States where this still happens.

The Miniature Train ride lasts about 10 minutes, and offers a very relaxing experience for families. Children love to be aboard and will beg to ride again once it ends. Purchase tickets for two rides in a row so you don't have to deboard and stand in line again. Benches are available for resting, eating lunch, or waiting in line, while nearby lawn areas provide a perfect spot for a picnic or afternoon snack. The sounds, movement, and color of the carousel and train are stimulating and exciting for very young children. There are restrooms nearby in Spanish Village.

San Diego Model Railroad Museum

The San Diego Model Railroad Museum opens a child's imagination to the world of miniatures, particularly scaled-down trains and railroad settings. Members of model railroad clubs all over San Diego have volunteered time building these sets. Young children are naturally fascinated by trains, and can look for specific items such as the railroad crossing signs or the lights in a station waiting room. Learning to observe finite details and focus on specific objects can be encouraged through an impromptu scavenger hunt as you move from installation to installation. (The volunteers offer a list of interesting and humorous things for older children to look for in the dioramas.) Near the lobby of the museum, a San Diego County relief map and touch screen computer monitor offer a three dimensional view of the local area. In one room children can actually operate toy trains. Children under four feet tall can stand on available step-stools, but smaller children will need to be held throughout the museum.

San Diego Natural History Museum

The San Diego Natural History Museum has fascinating traveling and permanent exhibitions, giant-screen films, and hands-on programs for all ages. One of its most popular exhibits for families is "Fossil Mysteries" which showcases the last 75 million years of changing life and landscape in southern California and the Baja Peninsula. Children will see life-size prehistoric animals (including dinosaurs, giant sharks, and lions), observe and touch real fossils, and enjoy interactive activities. Visitors can explore, discover, investigate and solve mysteries using handouts and a simulated paleontological excavation.

There are other exhibits with exploratory resources and life-like environments. On Sunday afternoons, Ms. Frizzle™, of The Magic School Bus© fame (Scholastic Publishing's children's book series and PBS television program), makes an appearance with an interactive presentation on a natural history topics of interest to little ones, i.e., bugs, dinosaurs, bats, etc. She involves children from the audience in her "Wacky Science" presentation. Her show is included in the cost of admission.

San Diego Zoo

Beginning at a very young age, children have a natural affinity for the Zoo. They delight in being strolled through the grounds, noticing everything from the hoots of a siamong to the twerps of an exotic bird. The San Diego Zoo is world-famous because of the natural settings created for the animals, which are enhanced by an extremely interesting botanical collection.

Planning a visit with your child's favorite animals in mind is the most educational and exciting way to explore the Zoo. You can access the Zoo's map on their Web site: **www.sandiegozoo.org/zoo/zoo_map.html** and plan a route prior to your visit.

> You can access the Zoo's map on their Web site...and plan a route prior to your visit.

The Children's Zoo, and especially the animal nursery, is a good spot to begin or end a trip to the Zoo. The newest Zoo babies are often on display in the nursery. Nearby, farmyard favorites roam in an open petting yard. All children love the "Mouse House" made out of a loaf of bread.

Visitor services for families include specialized tours, stroller rentals, snack bars and restaurants, frequently placed restrooms with good baby-changing facilities, gift shops, and double-deck buses to save walking. Plan your day around two animal shows: the Wegeforth Bowl sea lion show and another, currently titled "The Wild Ones," which showcases predators and prey from around the world. Check the schedule at the entrance and ask about other special events or enclosure changes.

Pepper Grove Discovery Playground and Picnic Area

Be sure to try out the Pepper Grove Discovery Playground. Not only will you find neat hands-on outdoor play equipment and experiments for kids to use and learn from, there are plenty of picnic tables in the shade and rolling lawn areas for playing games. With adjacent parking and restrooms nearby, this has naturally become a popular birthday party spot. Parents will enjoy the views across the canyon to the Organ Pavilion and California Tower beyond.

Balboa Park December Nights

A major event in San Diego, labeled Balboa Park's gift to the community, is "December Nights." Attending this event is a wonderful way for a family to celebrate the holiday season. Bundle up at night, listen to the carolers, smell roasting chestnuts, stroll through the museums, and eat foods from around the world sold at the museums and the international cottages of the House of Pacific Relations.

Young children may especially enjoy a Santa Lucia procession at the Museum of Man where Swedish youth, dressed in traditional white robes, parade through the museum singing traditional Swedish Christmas songs. In another area, San Diego Junior Theatre actors perform parts from past and future musical plays for all to enjoy. Most of the activities are free, including the museums (evenings only).

Especially for older kids...

Reuben H. Fleet Science Center

The Science Center always offers amazing displays that get a "wow" reaction from my kids. Thematically designed interactive exhibits examine scientific concepts. Changing exhibits are usually displayed downstairs, while upstairs smaller galleries showcase longer-term exhibits. The Demonstration Station is upstairs, and there is also a demonstration that travels through the building with Exhibit Interpreters. Topics range from biology to physics.

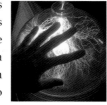

Groups can reserve the Nierman Challenger Learning Center with simulated voyages to Mars or the Moon. These are planned for groups of 20 or more students in grade 5 and above with prior reservations. Public missions are also available, offering an opportunity for family groups to participate.

San Diego Air and Space Museum

This museum offers a great place for a living history lesson. From the earliest hot air balloon flights of late 18th century France to modern-day space shuttles orbiting high above the earth, the colorful story of aviation unfolds as you walk through the exhibits.

Elaborate sets depict World War II when Spitfires, Me 109s, Zeros and Hellcats fought to rule the skies over Europe and the Pacific Ocean. Even the flight deck of an aircraft carrier—the Yorktown—has been recreated to simulate the conditions on board. These and accurately restored aircraft from the Korean and Vietnam conflicts reflect the increasingly complex technology used in modern warfare.

Kids of all ages can take a ride on a flight simulator and see what it feels like to fly a Sopwith Camel or a P-51 Mustang; land an F-18 on the deck of the USS Constellation or take a simulated walk in space. There is an additional charge for this at the Admission's Desk.

Docents give tours of the restoration areas in the huge basement with advance reservations. Most of the aircraft displayed in the museum are in mint condition because knowledgeable volunteers have assembled them. Many are retired aerospace manufacturing employees. They love to talk about the work they do, and an hour spent here will be well remembered. In addition to museum admission, there is a small fee for the tour.

San Diego Automotive Museum

The Automotive Museum has an extensive collection of automobiles and a general display on automotive history. They offer a program for school groups on "Women in Automotive History," and there's a teaching room with a cut-a-way of an operable engine—a Buick Le Sabre. A connection can be made to local history with a display of board planks laid out in the style of a historical road once running across the sand dunes just west of Yuma, Arizona.

San Diego Hall of Champions

The San Diego Hall of Champions is the nation's largest multi-sport museum, boasting three levels of memorabilia and 68,000 square feet. The museum offers a state-of-the-art theater, an interactive media center and fascinating displays on the nation's favorite sports. Exhibits deal not only with San Diego sports history but provide opportunities for interactive, hands-on experiences for youth and adults.

San Diego Museum of Man

The Museum of Man has many exhibits that will hold the interest of children. "Discover Egypt" is an interactive space designed as two types of homes from ancient Egypt. With replicated costumes, furniture, games, and simulated archaeological excavations, you can explore the lives of farmers and nobility.

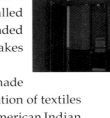

While at this anthropology museum don't miss a fascinating, interactive exhibit about evolution, called "Footsteps in Time." This recent addition was funded in part by the National Science Foundation and makes the complex topic more approachable for all ages.

On the main floor, visitors can taste hand-made traditional Mexican tortillas or see a live demonstration of textiles woven on an upright loom. The museum hosts an American Indian Fair each June that features dance groups, top quality artisans, traditional foods, and a crafts' corner for children.

Spanish Village, Pottery Guild, Gem & Mineral Society

Spanish Village houses artists' workshops and studios for the Pottery Guild and the San Diego Gem & Mineral Society. Artisans demonstrate their work, allowing children an opportunity to watch artisans blowing glass, throwing a pot, tumbling gems, or making jewelry. Most studios have one-of-a-kind items on view and items for sale. Hold back exploring hands, and let each artist know your family would love to see a demonstration.

The San Diego Gem & Mineral Society displays many specimens of interest to children. There are fossils from local digs, colorful geodes, and sparkling minerals, as well as demonstrations of gem and stone polishing and jewelry making. On Saturday mornings, from 10 a.m.-1 p.m., the Junior Gem and Mineral Society allows children 12 years and older to try their hand at polishing and setting stones.

San Diego Junior Theatre

San Diego Junior Theatre performances are a delight for children and adults. The actors are children 8-18 years old who have previously participated in the Junior Theatre's education programs. Programming includes a variety of plays and musicals each season, ranging from Shakespeare to classic children's literature and popular musicals. Children also produce all the behind-the-scenes work, i.e., lighting, sound, scene changes, costumes, and props. Volunteers raising funds for the organization sell snacks and drinks during a 15-minute intermission. Restrooms are inside the theater. Show tickets may be purchased in advance.

Museum of Photographic Arts

Photography is a great way to introduce a young person to the arts. The Museum of Photographic Arts (MoPA) in Balboa Park is a nationally recognized museum, offering access to the work of some of the best photographers in the world. Children under 12 are admitted free; adult admission prices are very reasonable. The Mandell Weiss Learning Center offers many public programs, including Photography Family Days with hands-on art-making activities and photographic workshops. Call the museum for specific times and information.

San Diego Museum of Art

Budding artists and art historians will want to put the San Diego Museum of Art at the top of their list of museums to visit. There is a renowned collection of European and American art, and a fine gallery of Asian art. The museum's Web site at: www.sdmart.org may be accessed in advance of your visit in order to plan a customized tour.

The Image Gallery is a good starting place for families. It's easy to plan a personalized tour through the collections by using a computer to access a database that includes 300 of the Art Museum's pieces with information about the artists. Visitors may select specific pieces or artists' work they would like to view, and print out their own tour of the galleries. For a nominal additional fee in the museum gift shop, you can even print out a computer reproduction of your favorite artwork to take home.

The Museum has several special annual events, including one in the spring that older children will enjoy, called "Art Alive." This unique display of flower arrangements, which interpret specific pieces of art, is a delight to the senses and an enjoyable way to view the galleries. Call for specific times of events.

Museum of San Diego History & Archives

The Historical Society offers great resources for students of all ages. A trip through the ever-changing exhibit galleries of the main museum or a docent tour of the George White and Anna Gunn Marston House (open Friday through Sunday only) on the west side of Balboa Park can bring history alive for elementary age kids. The emphasis is on San Diego's colorful past, but connections to broader lessons at school will be apparent. Apart from the house itself, the formal gardens of the Marston House, dating back to the 1920s, offer young children a nice place for exploration. (The gardens are free and open every day.)

...the formal gardens of the Marston House, dating back to the 1920s, offer young children a nice place for exploration.

Families can peruse historic photos of their own neighborhood in the Society's Research Archives where a vast collection of not just photos but scrapbooks are kept. Oral histories are also available and would make a great subject for a term paper for an older student. Volunteers are available to assist with the research. There is a small fee to use the archives; a modest admission is charged for the museums. (Visit both museums for one fee.)

CHAPTER 10
ANNUAL FESTIVALS/SPECIAL EVENTS

Balboa Park, as the cultural heart of San Diego, hosts some of the city's most important festivals and annual celebrations. In addition, the gentle climate makes it possible to hold special events of all sizes year-round, with something for just about everyone. Although the event schedule for the Park is constantly updated with new offerings, the following list comprises most of the ones that have developed a track record and a following over the years.

Annual Ethnic Food Fair booth

Generally these events are free and held around the same time each month/year unless otherwise noted; however, this schedule is subject to change. If in doubt, check with the Balboa Park Visitors Center, the Park Administration Center or the sponsoring organization. (Listed chronologically by weekday or month.)

Sundays at the International Cottages

Every Sunday afternoon from 12 noon to 4 p.m., the individually decorated International Cottages of the House of Pacific Relations, open their doors to Park visitors. See native arts and crafts and sample pastries from around the world; donations suggested. Also from February through mid-November, enjoy a lawn program of folk-dancing or singing by members in traditional costumes at 2 p.m., sponsored by one of the countries represented. To check schedule of lawn programs, call the Balboa Park Visitors Center: (619) 239-0512 Web site: **www.balboapark.org/events**

Spreckels Organ Concerts — Sundays

Rain or shine, these free concerts take place on the world's largest outdoor pipe organ at 2 p.m. on Sundays year-round. This historic instrument was dedicated on New Year's Eve 1914 by its donor John D. Spreckels, and has provided musical enjoyment for generations of San Diegans ever since. San Diego's civic organist, or one of many guest organists from around the world, performs a variety of musical programs. Sponsored by the Spreckels Organ Society: (619) 702-8138. Web site: **www.sosorgan.com**

Art Mart — Saturdays & Sundays

On the first and third weekends each month, the Balboa Park Craftsman Council hosts art shows on the lawn near the Federal Building. The bi-monthly Art Mart, which is sponsored by the Park and Recreation Department, features the work of local artists and craftspersons in an informal outdoor setting. Saturdays and Sundays 9 a.m. to 4 p.m. at President's Way and Pan American Plaza. Admission is free but items are available for purchase. Call (619) 235-1100 for current info or a contact name.

10K Runs — Saturdays & Sundays

Averaging two per month, year-round, these runs take place along an accredited racing course through the Balboa Park's most scenic areas. Many also include a 5K Run/Walk component. Races usually start and finish early on a Saturday or Sunday morning in the Pan American Plaza parking lot. Largest annual events include the Project Wildlife Run and Dr.

Seuss Run for Literacy. Fees benefit sponsoring organizations. Call the Park Administration Center for current schedule and registration information: (619) 235-1100.

African Drumming — Sundays, Tuesdays and Fridays

Free classes are offered for children on Sundays from 4 to 5 p.m.; for a modest fee, West African drumming lessons are given on Tuesdays from 3 to 4:15 p.m. (two age levels offered). On Fridays, African drumming classes for all ages are offered from 5 to 6 p.m., for around $10. Most classes are on a drop-in basis and are held at the WorldBeat Center. Additional classes are available weekly in Egyptian drumming, Brazilian samba and African dance. Times and fees vary. Call (619) 230-1190 or (best bet) log on to: **www.worldbeatcenter.org** for more details.

Free Tuesdays

Almost every week, year-round, several museums open their doors free of charge. Generally only the museum's permanent collection is available for viewing; special exhibitions and films may be excluded. An adult must accompany children under 12. The schedule rotates among the museums (subject to change). **To check current schedule, call the Balboa Park Visitors Center: (619) 239-0512.**

- **First Tuesdays:** Centro Cultural de la Raza; Model Railroad Museum; Natural History Museum; Reuben H. Fleet Science Center

- **Second Tuesdays:** Museum of Photographic Arts; Museum of San Diego History; Veterans Museum and Memorial Center

- **Third Tuesdays:** Art Institute, Japanese Friendship Garden; Mingei International Museum; Museum of Art; Museum of Man

- **Fourth Tuesdays:** Air and Space Museum; Automotive Museum; Hall of Champions. Also some of the International Cottages of the House of Pacific Relations are open, and a free film entitled, "Children around the World" is usually shown between 11 a.m. and 3 p.m., at the Hall of Nations.

- **Fifth Tuesdays:** Museums are open, but charge regular admission fees.

NOTE: *Some museums now admit only active-duty military and San Diego County residents for free. If you're an out-of-town visitor, call the Visitors Center (619-239-0512) or check* **www. balboapark.org** *for info on current Free Tuesdays policy.*

First Wednesdays

Two events now take place each month on the first Wednesday. In conjunction with a monthly astronomy lecture at the Reuben H. Fleet Science Center, telescopes of all sizes are set up by members of the San Diego Astronomy Association, weather permitting. Small fee for lecture (free for members), no charge for assisted night-sky viewing. Telescopes are set up outside the museum near the fountain on the Plaza de Balboa usually by 7:30 p.m. For more info: (619) 238-1233.

The San Diego Museum of Art hosts an evening of Jazz in the Park on the first Wednesday of each month, usually held in the Sculpture Garden. No host bar and hors d'oeuvres available from the menu at Waters Café. Admission fee. In case of inclement weather, the event is held in the adjacent Copley Auditorium. For more info: (619) 232-7931.

Museum Month — February

February is Museum Month in San Diego, offering another chance to see not only the museums in Balboa Park, but also others throughout the city, at a low cost.

Pick up a "culture card," usually at one of the big department stores in town (check with the Visitors Center or any of the museums to find out which company is participating this year), and have your discount card punched or stamped as you tick off each museum you visit. The program is organized by the San Diego Museum Council. Understandably, certain restrictions apply. Museum Month is a great program designed to give you a taste of the rich assortment of cultural offerings available in San Diego. For more info, contact the Museum Council office, (619) 231-1640, or check with the Visitors Center in February.

Dance Collage Concert — February

Incorporating a different theme each year, the San Diego Civic Dance Company performs in concert for two weeks in February each year. These talented young people must audition to participate in the performing group of forty to fifty dancers that make up the Company. Performances take place at the Casa del Prado Theater. Ticket prices are very reasonable; sales support the non-profit organization. For event information, call the Balboa Park Visitors Center in February: (619) 239-0512. For further information about any of the Park and Recreation Department dance programs, call (619) 525-8258.

International Dance Festival — February

International dance groups demonstrate folk and ballroom dancing from around the world. Enjoy an afternoon of native costumes, crafts, ethnic foods and vendor booths. Takes place at the Balboa Park Club from 12 noon to 5 p.m. Free. For more info: call (619) 286-1588, or check the Visitors Center in February for more information. Also check **www.idasdc.org**.

St. Patrick's Day Parade — March

On the Saturday closest to St. Patrick's Day, the west side of Balboa Park celebrates life on the Emerald Isle. The fun begins with a parade through the surrounding neighborhood, ending at Sixth Avenue and Laurel Street for a day-long Irish Festival. The festival includes an assortment of bands, Irish dance performances, food and other vendors-including a "Green Beer Garden." Parade starts at Sixth Avenue and Juniper Street around 11 a.m. Festival takes place between Nutmeg and Laurel Streets on the lawn areas along Sixth Avenue. Festival grounds open at 10 a.m. Call (858) 268-9111 or (619) 299-7812.

Earth Fair — April

This major event is always held on the Sunday closest to Earth Day (usually the second weekend in April). Balboa Park is transformed into an environmental fair with over two hundred booths, musical groups and activities promoting better stewardship of the Earth.

Billed as the largest free environmental fair in the Western U.S., Earth Fair in San Diego   typically draws over 60,000 attendees. Public transportation, foot and/or pedal-power are recommended. Parking is at a premium and traffic is usually grid-locked. In addition, the use of public transportation honors the spirit of Earth Day. Hours: 10 a.m. to 5 p.m. Location: booths are set up on Village Place (behind the Natural History Museum), along El Prado, Plaza de Panama, Pan American Road, and at the Organ Pavilion. Contact: San Diego EarthFair organizers, (858) 272-7370; website: **www.earthdayweb.org**

Greater San Diego Science & Engineering Fair — March/April

San Diego has a deserved reputation as a high-tech community. To get a glimpse of the up and coming young talent in the community, don't miss this annual event. Budding scientists and engineers, from 7th to 12th grades throughout San Diego County, present their annual science fair projects each year in Balboa Park. Nearly 1,000 students compete for scholarships and other prizes. Many go on to win state and even national competitions. Topics range from marine biology to computer engineering.

Nearly 1,000 students compete for scholarships and other prizes.

Judging takes place on the first day; displays are open for public viewing over the next three days, usually through the following weekend. Event takes place at the Balboa Park Activity Center on Park Boulevard at Inspiration Point Way. Parking is available at the Inspiration Point lots at President's Way and Park Boulevard. For more information, call (619) 293-2115, or check **www.gsdsef.org**

American Indian Cultural Days — May

Featuring traditional singers and dancers, American Indian food, and arts and crafts booths, this colorful event usually takes place on the third weekend in May at the corner of President's Way and Park Blvd. Free. Plenty of parking nearby in the Inspiration Point parking lots across the street. For more information and specific dates, call (619) 281-5964.

Ethnic Food Fair — May

Always held on the last Sunday in May, this delectable food fest is a major fundraising event for the International Cottages of the House of Pacific Relations. Sample foods from around the world while supporting the regular volunteer activities of the member groups sponsoring the cottages. Thirty-one countries are represented. Come early and expect long lines at the most popular food booths. Location: International Cottages of the House of Pacific Relations, corner of President's Way and Pan American Road. Hours: 11 a.m. to 5 p.m. Admission free, food prices vary.

Fern Street Circus — May

Each year in Balboa Park, the Fern Street Circus stages a new and spectacular show featuring local circus and variety artists in a simple and whimsical setting. The lively show has plenty of acrobatics, dance and "gravity-defying" moments, accompanied by original music performed by a live band. Performances mix adult artists with teens and children taught in an after school program. Takes place over two weekends with matinee and evening performances. Location: corner of President's Way and Park Boulevard. Tickets are very reasonable.

Founded in 1990 as a theatrical and educational circus ensemble, the non-profit organization is committed to teaching children motor skills, discipline, self-worth, and the joy of learning. Year-round after school programs take place at the Golden Hill Recreation Center on the east side of Balboa Park. Proceeds from the public performances in May support their educational programs. Call (619) 237-9756, or log on to **www.fernstreetcircus. org** for more info.

Annual Indian Fair — June

American Indians from around the U.S. gather at the Museum of Man over the second weekend in June, to demonstrate tribal dances and sell arts, crafts and ethnic food. More than 100 performers and artists representing dozens of tribes perform throughout the weekend. Proceeds benefit the tribes represented. Hours: Usual museum hours are observed. Fee: regular admission to museum. Call (619) 239-2001.

Annual Gay & Lesbian Pride Parade and Festival — July

San Diego's sizable gay and lesbian community stages this two-day festival at Marston Point on the Park's west side. Festivities start late Saturday morning with a colorful parade down Sixth Avenue. Festival includes food, booths, children's activities and entertainment. Location: Parade starts at University Avenue & Normal Street, in Hillcrest, and proceeds down Sixth Avenue to the Park; gated festival grounds are located at Marston Point, near Sixth & Juniper. Hours: Parade, 12 noon, Saturday; Festival, 2-10 p.m., Saturday; 12-9 p.m., Sunday. Fee charged for entry to the festival grounds. Call (619) 297-7683 for specific dates and other info.

Summer Twilight Concerts — June, July & August

Tuesday, Wednesday and Thursday summer evenings bring a variety of musical styles to the Spreckels Organ Pavilion stage— everything from barbershop quartets to Big Band sounds. Annual favorites include the U.S. Navy Band, Sun Harbor Men's Chorus, and the San Diego Youth Swing Band. These one-hour concerts are free, family-oriented, and definitely picnic-worthy. Location: Spreckels Organ Pavilion. Hours: 6:15 - 7:15 p.m. Free. Info: (619) 239-0512.

Summer Organ Festival Concerts — June, July & August

From mid-June through August each year, the Spreckels Organ Society presents its annual International Summer Organ Festival, featuring eminent theater and church organists from throughout the world, sometimes accompanied by other instrumentalists or vocalists. Musical styles range from classical to pop. Some of the concerts are themed to the season (i.e., the concert closest to July 4th features a patriotic theme). These delightful events take place on Monday evenings—a quiet, relaxed time in Balboa Park. No problems finding parking or picnic space. Hours: Mondays, mid-June to late August, 7:30 p.m. Location: Spreckels Organ Pavilion. Free. (619) 702-8138. **www.sosorgan.com**

Philippine Cultural Arts Festival — August

Celebrating San Diego's thriving Filipino community, this two-day festival features concerts, artists and indigenous foods. The festivities take place from 11 a.m. to 6 p.m., usually on the first weekend in May. Location: On the lawn area at President's Way and Park Boulevard. Free. Call (619) 444-7528 for more details.

Oktoberfest (Folk Dance Festival) — September

This two-day event takes place at the Balboa Park Club on one of the last weekends in September. Beginners' workshops are held on Saturday. On Sunday you can participate or just watch dancers in colorful ethnic costumes dance to the music of many countries. Join in hourly free dance lessons—partners not required. Besides the dance exhibitions, expect food, folk and dance vendors. Admission is free. Call (619) 286-1588 or log onto **www.idasdc.org** for more info.

Founder's Day at the Zoo — October

The San Diego Zoo does not participate in the Free Tuesdays program but does open its gates to the public one day a year on Founder's Day—the first Monday in October— in honor of Zoological Society founder Harry Wegeforth. Needless to say, thousands of people turn out for this event, creating traffic jams on the main thoroughfares and on Zoo walkways. But it's a wonderful opportunity to visit one of the world's greatest Zoos at no charge. Hours: Regular Zoo operating hours, first Monday in October only. Location: San Diego Zoo.

Fiesta de la Cuadrilla — November

Sponsored by the San Diego Square Dance Association, over 1000 participants from all over Southern California and elsewhere, dance for fun on the first full weekend of November. During workshops, hundreds of dancers learn 140 different moves for varying skill levels. Round dances for couples are also performed. Although not a competitive event, there is a modest fee charged to participate. Door prizes are awarded. Colorful costumes, foot-tapping music and enthusiasm that is catching, will delight spectators who can observe for free! Event takes place indoors in various Park facilities. Information: (858) 277-6621.

Balboa Park December Nights — December

Every year most of the museums of Balboa Park open their exhibit halls free of charge on the first Friday and Saturday nights in December for this huge celebration—the largest free public event in San Diego. The museums are only free from 5 to 9 p.m., but there are very special entertainment and food offerings both days. The event typically draws over 100,000 people each night, but in many ways retains a charming, homespun holiday atmosphere. Hours: Fri., 5-10 p.m.; Sat., noon to 10 p.m. Location: along the Prado; the Palisades area, Spanish Village, and at the Spreckels Organ Pavilion.

CHAPTER 11
"TOP TEN" SPOTS IN BALBOA PARK

Volunteers at the Balboa Park Visitors Center are continually amazed to hear people say they had no idea "all this was here." In some cases, these first-time visitors have lived in San Diego for several years, and never ventured outside the Zoo on a trip to Balboa Park. Tourists have been told they shouldn't miss Balboa Park, but have no idea what to expect once they arrive. Many people never venture off the main walkways and consequently miss some of the most charming aspects of the Park.

Summer picnic and a concert in Bird Park

Depending on what you're looking for, the top ten spots vary. Therefore, we've compiled a "top ten" list of our favorite spots for romance, picnics, and souvenirs—photo and otherwise.

These lists are, of course, subjective. Depending on one's area of interest, you could come up with a completely different compilation! Please send us your favorite spots for possible inclusion in future editions (to be updated every year or so). Just e-mail editor@balboaparkguide.com, or fax your suggestions to (619) 255-9888.

10 hidden treasures

Following is a list of very special places one should see to have a more complete picture of Balboa Park. It does not contain the obvious favorites—major cultural institutions (although a few are located within major attractions), buildings and gardens—but rather some not-so-obvious choices.

1. St. Francis Chapel—Museum of Man

A surprising find in the heart of the Park, this chapel has been in existence since the 1915 Exposition when it was built to recreate the elaborate interior of a Spanish mission church in early California. When the Park served as an extension of the Naval Hospital during World War II, it became the site of many weekend weddings before a sailor shipped out, and has been used for this purpose occasionally ever since. Admission to the museum is required.

2. Balboa Park Club

Fashioned after a famous 16th century mission church from the Southwest, complete with irregular walls and rough-hewn beams, the Balboa Park Club was built for the 1915 Exposition as an exhibit hall for the State of New Mexico. In 1935, it was extensively renovated to become the Palace of Education, and during World War II, served as a Naval Officers Club. Today you can get a sense of the building's colorful history by stepping inside to consider the murals, historic fountain and photographs. Located across from the International Cottages of the House of Pacific Relations near Pan American Plaza

3. Bird Park

This recent, unheralded addition to the northeast corner of the Park is one of the prettiest spots in the area, and the best place to fly a kite. Creatively landscaped to resemble a bird with its nest of eggs from a "bird's eye view," it will delight kids and adults alike. In the summer, great free concerts in many different styles take place here weekly. Located at 28th and Upas Streets.

4. Palm Canyon

A botanical treasure trove worth seeking out on a hot day, you'll feel like you're entering another world. Dating back to the early 1900s, over 450 palms of 58 different varieties have been imported and planted here. There is a short hiking trail that leads to the Balboa Park Club. Enter the canyon from a wooden footbridge, just off Pan American Road near the Alcazar Garden parking lot.

5. George and Anna Gunn Marston House

Set apart from the other museums, in the northwest corner of the Park, is an historic gem: the Marston House and Gardens, dating back to 1905. Constructed in the Craftsman style for successful merchant, civic leader and Balboa Park activist George W. Marston, and his wife Anna, the home harkens back to life in San Diego prior to the two Expositions in Balboa Park. Open for docent tours Fri.-Sun., 10 a.m.- 5 p.m. Modest admission is charged.

6. Courtyard of House of Hospitality

The Park has many quiet corners, but this one is a must for every visitor. The House of Hospitality, one of the most important buildings in the Park, was reconstructed in the late 1990s, garnering many awards for its historic authenticity. The fountain and courtyard date back to the 1935 Exposition when architect Richard Requa modeled it after a museum in Guadalajara, Mexico.

7. The Old Bridle Trail

Used primarily by local residents who live around the Park, this little known hiking and biking trail was in fact developed for equestrian use between the World Wars. Except for traffic noise from State Highway 163, you could be in the backcountry of San Diego County, amid flowering trees, squirrels and birds. There are three ways to access the trail: from Upas Street near Richmond just west of the Boy Scout headquarters; from the Redwood Circle area near the lawn bowling courts; or from the northwest corner of the Park near the Marston House Museum and Gardens. (*Approximately two miles round-trip under moderately strenuous conditions.*)

8. House of Pacific Relations/International Cottages

Cottages, representing 31 countries, are open every Sunday, 12 noon to 5 p.m. International goodies are available to sample, and folk dancing is performed on the outdoor stage at 2 p.m. from February through mid-November. Free admission. Also visit the United Nations Association Building, which is open every day. Located near President's Way and Pan American Road.

9. Spanish Village

Allow time to meander through this colorful enclave of artists studios located on Village Place between the museums of El Prado and the San Diego Zoo. Potters, enamel jewelry-makers, watercolorists and sculptors work and enjoy interacting with visitors here. Art pieces for sale. Folk musicians and face-painters often appear on weekends making this even more fun for children. Free.

10. Model Railroad Museum

Worth a stop for young and old alike, this is one of the largest scale-model train layouts in the nation! Over the years, volunteer model railroad enthusiasts have painstakingly created a very special environment down to the minutest detail for several different gauges of trains. Located in the basement of the Casa de Balboa. Modest admission fee; free for children under 15.

10 most romantic spots

With its fairytale architecture, green landscape, and variety of gardens and fountains, the name Balboa Park is synonomous with romance in San Diego. But within the Park there are some spots even more romantic than the next. This list includes several gardens, viewpoints, and restaurants—perfect places to while away an afternoon with someone special in your life.

1. Rose Garden

Except for two months in the early part of the year when the rose bushes are pruned back, this is one of the most romantic spots in the Park. Row upon row of fragrant, colorful roses, soothing fountains, and a quiet, shaded pergola also make this a very popular wedding spot. This beautiful garden features 2,500 rose bushes with nearly 200 varieties of colorful roses, usually at their peak bloom from late May through October.

2. Alcazar Garden

Unless you know where to find this gem, you may miss one of the loveliest spots in all of Balboa Park. Located between the House of Charm and the Museum of Man's south exhibit halls, sits a quiet retreat that conjures up images of southern Spain with its formal hedges and Moorish tiled fountains.

3. Sunken courtyard behind Museum of Man

This small, shaded court has a lovely fountain and benches; it sits off the beaten path in the shadow of the California Tower. Located between the Old Globe Theatre complex and the Museum of Man.

4. Marston House Gardens

Another popular wedding spot, these formal English gardens date back to the 1920s when the Marston family played an important role in the history of San Diego and Balboa Park. The gardens are located behind a Craftsman style home, now a historical museum (open for tours on weekends), which was designed by famed San Diego architect Irving Gill.

5. Zoro Garden

Secluded butterfly and wildflower garden in summer, this rock-walled amphitheater housed a nudist colony for the 1935 Exposition. Unless there is a free performance of Shakespeare, most likely you'll have this quiet enclave all to yourselves.

6. Timken Museum

Entering this elegant museum reminds one of European sojourns in centuries gone by. Inspirational setting for hand-holding and whispering while contemplating several Old Masters. Visitors from overseas know of its reputation and seek out the Timken's ambiance and high-quality collection of art from the Renaissance through the 19th century. Admission is free.

7. Marston Point

Bicycle or roller-skate along Balboa Drive to the end of the circular drive, and you'll be rewarded with some of the best views in the Park. This beautiful tree-lined walk was named for Park supporter George Marston. He and his wife Anna lived just a few blocks north of here. (Their home for 35 years before his death in 1941, is situated near the north end of Balboa Drive, at Upas Street and Seventh Avenue, and is now a historical museum.)

8. The Prado Restaurant/Casa del Rey Moro Gardens

The terraced gardens have probably been the site of more Balboa Park weddings than any other. Highly romantic spot with its wishing well and views into the surrounding landscape. The restaurant has a warm, inviting decor with cozy booths inside, views of the gardens and terraces outside. Located in the historic House of Hospitality.

9. Albert's Restaurant at the Zoo

Located in the Gorilla Tropics area of the San Diego Zoo, this restaurant has the feeling of a treetop safari retreat. Go after the lunch hour rush, or reserve a table during the early evening when "Nighttime Zoo" hours are in effect during the summer. Sit at a table by the window with the rushing waterfall outside and shuttered light falling across palm trees, and you'd swear you're in a distant tropical locale.

10. Aerial Tram at the Zoo

It's so quiet up here you can hear baboons barking and tigers roaring. But you also get breathtaking views of the city skyline, the California Tower, and lacy treetops of Balboa Park.

Hint: Balboa Park is one of San Diego's top wedding sites. Depending on the size and type of wedding you're planning, your event can be as inexpensive or elaborate as you wish.

For available outdoor locations, except the Marston House Gardens, call the Park Rangers, (619) 235-5900 (permits are required for groups of 75 or more). For weddings in the Marston House Gardens, call (619) 235-1105. To use the St. Francis Chapel at the Museum of Man (there is a fee), call (619) 239-2001.

For weddings and receptions in the private rooms at the House of Hospitality or in the terraced gardens behind the building, call (619) 232-9333. (Catering can only be provided by The Prado restaurant.)

Visit **www.balboapark.org** and link to the museums of your choice or call (619) 231-9494 and ask about facility reservations.

10 best picnic spots

There are no limits to possible picnic spots, but there are some areas that especially lend themselves to a relaxing meal in the open. Whether you're entertaining someone special, or just want to get the family out of doors this weekend, pack a picnic or pick up your favorite take-away foods, and use the enclosed map with the list below, to help you find just the right spot.

Just a few rules apply: **alcoholic beverages may be consumed only in the Central Mesa area of the Park between 8 a.m. and 8 p.m.** No glass containers or open fires are allowed in the Park. It's okay to bring a small grill and barbecue in the Park, but you must dispose of ashes carefully in designated containers (located in the main picnic areas). Be considerate of others. No amplified music. Remove all trash, leaving the area as clean or cleaner than you found it. Recycle aluminum cans.

For larger groups: Morley Field group picnic area; along Sixth Avenue; at President's Way and Park Blvd., or at the Veteran's War Memorial Building lawn area. Check with Balboa Park Administration Center staff for availability; permit needed for group larger than 75. Call (619) 235-1104.

1. Sixth Avenue/Quince Street/Redwood Circle

Rolling lawns, picnic tables, tall evergreen trees with views of the California Tower beyond—even tree squirrels imported by the Zoo in the early 1900s—complete the atmosphere. All make this a perfect place to spread a picnic. Afterwards visit the historic Marston House museum on Seventh Avenue, or go bike riding or skating south along the Balboa Drive loop down to Marston Point and back. *(Picnic tables; children's playground; public outdoor restrooms nearby.)*

2. Pepper Grove Discovery Playground

Set in a grove of shady California and Brazilian pepper trees, it's the perfect setting for an outdoor family meal with young children, complete with whimsically painted picnic tables and state-of-the-art playground equipment. Located on Park Boulevard south of the Reuben Fleet Science Center. *(Plenty of picnic tables, children's playground, public outdoor restroom nearby.)*

3. Bird Park

The best place in the Park to fly a kite, it's also one of the best-kept secrets in Balboa Park. Rolling lawns with views of downtown San Diego in the distance, new play equipment and an artistic landscaping theme. In the summer, great free concerts in many different styles take place here weekly. Located near the Morley Field Sports Complex in the northeast corner of the Park at Upas Street and Pershing Drive. (*Some picnic tables, children's playground, public outdoor restroom nearby.*)

4. Activity Center Garden Court

A formal garden courtyard between the modern Activity Center and the old Naval Hospital's historic landmark building, has been effectively landscaped and developed to blend the old and the new. Today the lovely, old pink building with the twin towers, functions as the Balboa Park Administration Center. All around it are formally landscaped walkways, benches and fountains. Some have been historically reconstructed. (*Nearest restrooms in the adjacent Balboa Park Activity Center.*)

5. Zoro Garden

Formerly the site of a popular nudist colony exhibit during the 1935 Exposition, today this secluded, sunken rock-walled amphitheater (between the Reuben H. Fleet Science Center and the Casa de Balboa) provides the perfect spot for a special occasion picnic. Planted as a wildflower and butterfly garden, it's an especially colorful retreat in spring and summer. (*Rock walls for seating; restrooms in the adjacent buildings; trailhead for moderate after-lunch hike nearby.*)

6. Moreton Bay Fig

A perfect spot for a traditional family picnic with blanket, basket, deviled eggs and homemade fried chicken, this shady lawn area is situated between the Natural History Museum and Spanish Village. Children's Carousel and Miniature Train are nearby. Village Grill snack bar on opposite corner offers traditional fast-food fare and towering frosty ice cream cones. (*Benches; nearest public restrooms in Spanish Village.*)

7. Alcazar Garden

With stunning views of the California Tower, this formal Moorish garden lends itself to a formal picnic with chilled wine, fancy breads and cheeses. Stunning views of California Tower. Flower boxes surrounded by hedges limit seating and privacy, but make this one of the most photogenic spots in the Park. (*Benches for seating; closest public restrooms are across the nearby parking lot.*)

8. Golden Hill Park

One of the oldest, developed areas of the Park, this area is well-used by local residents but not generally known to other Park visitors. Since the surrounding neighborhood has been enjoying a renaissance, this area of the Park, somewhat neglected until recently, will be restored in the near future. Contains some of the most unusual botanical treasures in the Park —including two very climbable Moreton Bay Fig Trees— and beautiful views of downtown and the bay beyond. (*Public restroom and picnic tables.*)

9. International Cottages/ Balboa Park Club lawn area

Great spot for a family picnic after a puppet show, or champagne fete for two before an evening performance at Starlight Bowl. This nice open lawn area, surrounded by tall palm trees, is located near the intersection of President's Way and the Palisades parking lot. Sundays at 2 p.m. enjoy folk dancing on the International Cottage stage or a free concert on the nearby Spreckels Organ. (*Closest public restroom is between Air and Space Museum and Automotive Museum; indoor restrooms are also available at the San Diego Hall of Champions.*)

10. Botanical Building/Lily Pond

This is a popular spot for picnics because of its scenic location in front of the Botanical Building. Situated close to the major art institutions in the Park, this would be a great place to have a gourmet lunch or supper before or after taking in a very special exhibition. A well-traveled area, definitely not secluded. (*Grassy areas with a limited number of benches around the Lily Pond. Closest public restroom in the Casa del Prado and Casa de Balboa Buildings.*)

10 outstanding gift shops

With more one-of-a-kind items than you'd ever find in a suburban mall, a shopping paradise awaits the casual visitor and serious shopper alike. Almost every museum has a gift shop featuring specialty items relating to the theme of that museum's collection. Some offer real collector's items and artifacts. All have extensive book selections.

Balboa Park is the place to find an unusual gift item for the hard-to-shop-for person on your list. Aviation or automotive buff? The Air and Space or Automotive Museum shops may have just the thing. Interested in wildlife? Don't miss the Zoo and Natural History Museum stores. Art, photography, gardening, or history—there is truly something for everyone. The best part is the satisfaction you get from knowing that the proceeds from your purchase help the non-profit organization associated with it. Unless otherwise noted, shop hours are the same as the museum/institution's hours.

1. Mingei International Museum

A feast for the eyes, this gorgeous store offers coffee table art books, and one-of-a-kind collector's items, including bowls, dolls, hand-lacquered birds and animals, and wearable art including coats, dresses, silk shawls, vests and saris.

2. U.N. Association /Unicef Gift Shop

Located slightly off the beaten path, near the House of Pacific Relations' International Cottages, this shop offers an eclectic mix of items from around the world. From musical CDs featuring flamenco jazz from Latin America to European candies, this is a fun place to shop with children. They will especially enjoy a hand-painted alcove dedicated to UNICEF. All proceeds benefit the local chapter of the United Nations Association. Open daily 10 a.m. to 5 p.m.

3. Museum of Man

"Worry dolls", silver and turquoise jewelry and woven baskets echo the Native American themes of the museum. Interesting book selection and reasonable prices make this lovely store a must for serious shoppers.

4. Museum of Art

A classy shop with items inspired by the museum's collection, including framed prints, stylish home and desk accessories, jewelry, books and catalogs. One corner features highly-stylized children's books and art sets. Gift certificates are available. Closed on Mondays.

5. Natural History Museum

Shop for books, tapes, dinosaurs, and stuffed animals—all relating to the ecology of the Southwest in a soothing environment with nature sounds playing in the background. Main store located off the dramatic entry atrium; smaller shop on the lower level.

6. Reuben Fleet Science Center

Hands-on games and puzzles, telescopes, science toys, watches and clocks, plus a good selection of books and magazines handpicked by a knowledgeable staff. You'll have a hard time pulling your kids away from this one (or your spouse for that matter)!

7. San Diego Zoo

Not just one, but several shops, each with a different emphasis. Wonderful T-shirts and sweatshirts, in fact an entire line of clothing, as well as stuffed toys, books, stationery, and decorative pieces—most with a wildlife theme—are available in each shop. Very friendly, helpful staff.

8. Hall of Champions Sports Museum

What you'd expect, but done very well. This is the place to buy sports team memorabilia-at a good price and for a good cause! Besides local team merchandise, NFL team collectable footballs, coffee table books and children's books are featured.

9. Museum of San Diego History

Everything relating to San Diego's colorful history and the Historical Society's four museums. Victorian dolls and coloring books, antique jewelry, and the best local history book selection in the city.

10. Balboa Park Visitors Center

Balboa Park's numerous gardens are the theme in this small, but interesting shop that adjoins the Visitors Center. Besides books, postcards and memorabilia about Balboa Park, find windchimes, butterfly houses, and natural twig baskets made from gleaned materials in the Park. Probably the best tee-shirt prices in the Park—maybe San Diego!

10 classic photo spots in the Park

Balboa Park is endlessly photogenic, but there are some locations that seem to be photographed more than others. These are the classic photo spots. If you're a photography buff, invest in Andrew Hudson's **Photosecrets: Balboa Park** for detailed info on how to get the best shots of the Park, including a special section about the Zoo. (Available in the Balboa Park Visitors Center and at local camera stores.) But if you just brought along your "point-and-shoot" or a disposable camera, here are 10 locations sure to please the camera's eye.

As a rule of thumb, shoot your photos early in the morning or late in the day. Photos shot in the middle of the day will be flat and lack detail. (One exception is the lawn bowling area off of Laurel Street. The lawn bowlers only appear between 1 and 3 p.m. every day.)

(**Use map codes below to identify location on folded map in back of book.**)

1. **Alcazar Garden with California Tower in Background (D6)**

2. **El Prado from Plaza de Balboa steps looking west towards the California Tower (F6)**

3. **Botanical Building and Lily Pond from El Prado (F6)**

4. **California Tower at the Museum of Man from west side of Cabrillo Bridge (B6)**

5. **Organ Pavilion from base of El Cid statue (E6)**

6. **House of Hospitality or House of Charm with El Cid in foreground (E6)**

7. **Flower-filled windowboxes and doorways in Spanish Village (F5)**

8. **Reuben H. Fleet Science Center or Natural History Museum with Evenson Fountain or hedge roses in foreground (G6)**

9. **Lawn bowling from Laurel Street (usually between 1 and 3 p.m. only) (B6)**

10. **San Diego Air and Space Museum with jet aircraft in the foreground (C9)**

And finally, if you're not a photographer but want to take home a visual record of your visit, check out the postcards and note cards available at the Visitors Center. Or purchase Andrew Hudson's photo essay of **The Magic of Balboa Park**. You'll find most of the shots listed above and many more, beautifully presented.

Sources

Printed Media:
American Guide Series, *"A Guide to Balboa Park"*
  Association of Balboa Park Institutions, pamphlet, 1941
Christman, Florence *The Romance of Balboa Park.*
  San Diego Historical Society, 1985.
Fuller, Theodore W. San Diego Originals
  California Profiles Publications, 1987
Herman, Kenneth *"The Historic Spreckels Organ"*
  Spreckels Organ Society, pamphlet, 1995
Hudson, Andrew *PhotoSecrets: San Diego*
  PhotoSecrets Publishing, 1998
Kooperman, Evelyn L. *San Diego Trivia*
  Silvergate Publications, 1989
MacPhail, Elizabeth C. *Kate Sessions: Pioneer Horticulturist*
  San Diego Historical Society, 1976
Mendel, Carol *San Diego on Foot, 9th Edition*
  Carol Mendel 1994
Mertz, Susan J. *"Parkitecture"*
  San Diego Historical Society, spiral-bound booklet, 1991
Showley, Roger M. *"El Prado: The Avenue of Dreams"*
  (Diamond Jubilee Self-Guided Tour of Balboa Park's El Prado)
  San Diego Historical Society, pamphlet, 1990
Showley, Roger M. *Balboa Park: A Millennium History*
  Heritage Media Corporation, 1999

Videos:
Ofield, Jack, producer/director, "Balboa Park: The Magic City," 1994
  The Production Center for Documentary and Drama/SDSU
  KPBS/ Balboa Park Endowment Funds of The San Diego
  Foundation

Ofield, Jack, producer/director, "Postcards from the Fair: San Diego's
  1935 California Pacific International Exposition," 1996
  The Production Center for Documentary and Drama/SDSU
  KPBS/Balboa Park Endowment Funds of The San Diego
  Foundation

Web Sites:
Many organizations in Balboa Park have Web sites. The sites listed throughout the book were referred to again and again and proved to be valuable sources of information for this project.

Additional Resources:
Balboa Park Visitors Center
California Room of the San Diego Central Library
Committee of 100
House of Hospitality Association
San Diego Historical Society Archives
San Diego Park & Recreation Department, Balboa Park Administration

Final note: There are over 100 different organizations in Balboa Park whose contact information changes constantly. Most are run by volunteers. For current information on Balboa Park organizations, log on to **www.balboapark.org**, call the Balboa Park Visitors Center, (619) 239-0512, or call the Balboa Park Administration Center, (619) 235-1100.

IMAX® is a registered trademark of IMAX Corporation.
Frisbee® is a registered trademark of Wham-O, Inc.
Rollerblade® is a registered trademark of Rollerblade, Inc.
Ms. Frizzle™ and *The Magic School Bus©* are registered trademarks of Scholastic Publishing.

Photo Credits

Front cover: *Walking on Old Globe Theatre plaza* near the California Tower, Brett Shoaf, courtesy of Balboa Park Marketing.

Back cover: *Free tram entering Balboa Park* by Charles Crooks.

Inside black & white photographs (unless otherwise noted were taken by Charles Crooks):

Chapter 1: *California Bldg. dome*, p. 9, Brett Shoaf*; *Cabrillo Canyon, Balboa Park, c. 1903*, p. 13, San Diego Historical Society, Photography Collection; *Statue of Kate Sessions*, p. 14, Brett Shoaf*; *Opening day, 1915 Panama-California Exposition*, p. 16, SD Historical Society, Photography Collection; *Federal Building architectural detail*, p. 19; *Visitors leave* the Federal Building, 1935, p. 20, SD Historical Society, Photography Collection; Reuben H. Fleet Science Center architectural detail, p. 22; Old Globe complex sign; p. 23, Brett Shoaf*.

Chapter 2: Waters Café @ SDMA, p. 25, Brett Shoaf; Cabrillo Bridge from Nate's Point, p. 30; Tram crossing bridge, p. 31, Brett Shoaf*; Prado Restaurant entrance, p. 35; Tea Pavilion sign, p. 37; Dog and owner at Bird Park, p. 48.

Chapter 3: 'Woman of Tehuantepec' fountain at House of Hospitality, p. 53; golf clubs at Balboa Golf Course, p. 54; Balboa Park Administration Building, p. 68.

Chapter 4: Botanical Building, p. 73; Modern north entry of Natural History Museum, p. 75; House of Hospitality tower dressed up for the holidays, p. 77; Panda, p. 79, stock photo by Bradley Photography, iStock Photo.

Chapter 5: New and old blend in Balboa Park, p. 81, Brett Shoaf*; Marston House Museum, p. 83; House of Germany entry, p. 85; House of Charm, p. 86, Brett Shoaf*; Air and Space Museum, p. 91; Hall of Champions, p. 96; Museum of Man façade, p. 100; Zoo sign, p. 102; UN Association building, p. 107; Veterans Museum, p. 108; Old Globe Theatre, p. 110; Puppet Theater, p. 112; Organ Pavilion concert, p. 114.

Chapter 6: Lawn Bowling, p. 117, courtesy of Andrew Hudson,/ Photosecrets; Balboa Golf Course views of downtown, p. 118; Desert Garden, p. 121.

Chapter 7: Moreton Bay Fig Tree, p. 127; Old Cactus Garden view of Balboa Park Club, p. 129, Brett Shoaf*.

Chapter 8: House of Hospitality on the Plaza de Panama, p. 135, Joanne DiBona*; Casa del Prado ornamentation, p. 136; Balboa Park Club, p. 138; Museum of Art statues, p. 139; House of Charm tower, p. 141.

Chapter 9: Child on Carousel, p. 145, Brett Shoaf*; Kid City sign at RH Fleet Science Ctr., p. 147; Miniature Train ride, p. 148, Brett Shoaf*; Girl and dinosaur at Natural History Museum, p. 149; Lightning globe at Science Center, p. 151; Family Day sign at Museum of Man, p. 153.

Chapter 10: Ethnic Food Fair booth, p. 157, Brett Shoaf*.

Chapter 11: Summer Picnic and concert at Bird Park, p. 167.

Inside color photographs:

First color page: *Urban forest, Air & Space Museum exhibit, School field trip on the Prado,* and *Veterans Memorial fountain,* all by Charles Crooks.

Second page: *Zoro Gardens, Free Tuesday at the Fleet, Butterfly in Zoro Gardens, Centro Cultural de la Raza,* all by Charles Crooks.

Third page: *Palm Trees* and *Carole Williams, Civic Organist,* by Brett Shoaf*; *Lily Pond* and *Summer Sunday at the Organ Pavilion* by Charles Crooks.

Fourth page: *Marston House Gardens* by Brett Shoaf*; *Under an arcade in early morning;* and *Sunrise on the Prado* by Charles Crooks.

Fifth page: *Balboa Golf Course with view to downtown* and *Artist in Desert Garden* by Charles Crooks; *George Marston, seated* by Brett Shoaf*.

Sixth page: *Giraffes at Zoo* and *Blooming flowers* by Charles; *A quiet walk in the Desert Garden* by Brett Shoaf*.

Seventh page: *Botanical Building, Fountain finials, Old Navy Hospital fountain,* and *Persian Carpet fountain* by Charles Crooks; *Museum of Art figures* by Brett Shoaf*.

Eighth page: *Spanish Village* by Brett Shoaf*; *Navy runners* and *Rollerblading west of Cabrillo Bridge* by Charles Crooks; *Indian dancers at International Cottages* by Tim Stahl*.

*Courtesy of Balboa Park Marketing.

185

Acknowledgments

It doesn't seem possible that it has been almost six years since the first edition of Discover Balboa Park was published. Since then I have learned even more about Balboa Park and updated the book accordingly. Undoubtedly I have still overlooked something. For that I apologize. Because opportunities are constantly evolving, I am changing things right up to press time!

The first ambitious edition, most of which is incorporated in this second one, couldn't have happened without the input and encouragement of many knowledgeable folks. Florence Christman's and Roger Showley's books on the history were invaluable as was the San Diego Historical Society's archives and Web site. Richard Amero's contributions to that Web site and to Andrew Hudson's books were also very helpful. Since there seems to be a fair amount of friendly disagreement as to the architectural inspiration of the historic buildings, I relied on Roger Conlee's interviews with Art Historian Will Chandler for clarification.

I love to use guidebooks when I travel and have found their recommendations for places to stay and eat especially helpful in a strange city. I have included similar suggestions for places in and around Balboa Park. My subjective recommendations are based purely on research and experience. No special consideration, monetary or otherwise, influenced their inclusion in the book.

I am indebted to Park Ranger Kim Duclo; Debbie Petruzelli, Balboa Park Public Relations Manager; and Susy Creamer, Balboa Park Visitors Center Volunteer Coordinator, for several readings of the second edition and their suggestions to improve it. Mike Rodrigues, an Area II Manager for San Diego Park and Recreation, reviewed the sections on recreational facilities and special events, while Kathy Puplava, former Balboa Park horticulturist helped me update the chapter on horticulture. Thanks also to Kathleen Hasenauer and Paul Sirois, Balboa Park District Managers, who both reviewed a final mock-up.

Veteran writer Roger Conlee, who wrote the chapter on Park architecture, contributed to several other chapters and has been a friendly voice of support throughout; Mary Anderson, whose love and knowledge of Balboa Park go back to childhood, contributed not only the chapter on horticulture, but also valuable information on some of the cultural and recreational facilities. Charlene Baldridge, whom I know from her days at The Old Globe, was a natural to write about the performing arts scene in Balboa Park. Trevor Copenhaver drew the terrific map you'll find in the back of the book and Laurie Berg worked patiently with me on the design and production of this edition to make it more user-friendly. My husband, Ted, once again tackled the index.

Special thanks to board members of the House of Hospitality Association, all the volunteers and staff from the Balboa Park Visitors Center, and to David Kinney, Executive Director of the House.

Sadly, four inspiring Balboa Park advocates I knew and worked with over the years have died since the first edition was published: Ed McKellar, former Executive Director of the Aerospace Museum; Pat DeMarce, President of the Committee of 100; Pauline DesGranges, former Director of San Diego Park and Recreation; and Dr. Homer Peabody, civic leader and Balboa Park promoter. Their influence and impact on the Park cannot be quantified. These people were well-known, with considerable influence in our community. Two other people, not as well-known outside the Park, had an impact on our jewel just the same.

Inge Dickens was the Cultural Arts Manager for Balboa Park when she died unexpectedly in February 2003. I worked with her on programming for Christmas on the Prado and Exposition 2000. Those who have enjoyed the Twilight in the Park concert series, dance classes and events, Balboa Park December Nights, and many other free or inexpensive opportunities for children and adults offered through the Park and Recreation Department have benefited from her creativity and dedication.

Bob McGlade, who passed away in July of 2005, was both an arts organization employee and a volunteer in Balboa Park most of his adult life. I worked with Bob for years on the Board of the House of Hospitality and and later when he became a staff member at the Balboa Park Visitor

Center. At different times over the years, Bob was an employee of The Old Globe Theater and Starlight Musical Theater, a board member and fundraiser for the San Diego Performing Arts League and one of the founders of Christmas on the Prado (Balboa Park December Nights). Inge and Bob were both instrumental in helping me finish the first edition of Discover Balboa Park, as much with encouragement as with suggestions. I really miss them as I finish this second edition, and am grateful for their contributions to me and to Balboa Park.

On a happier note, we now live right next to America's Greatest Urban Park. What a special gift from a very hard-working and supportive spouse. Thanks, Ted, for this...and 30 wonderful years.

The author

Index

Other popular **Ridgway Park** products include:

Kate Sessions:
Mother of Balboa Park
$10.95

*In this charming children's book, author and illustrator **Joy Raab** tells how San Diego's unique urban park became a botanical, as well as cultural wonderland. **Kate Sessions: Mother of Balboa Park** chronicles the story of Kate's life from her days as a student in Oakland in the late 1800s, to her proudest moment when, at age 81, she received a medal from the American Genetic Association - first ever awarded to a woman - for her work in flower and plant introduction.*

A Walk in Balboa Park 1 & 2
$3.95 each

Walking is one of the best things about being in Balboa Park. These convienient pocket-sized books have a handy central map and insights into the history, buildings, major botanical gardens and various other features of the Park.

*Now you can tour the Park with **Pam Crooks**, author of **Discover Baloa Park**!*

Balboa Park Map & Trail Guide
$3.00 each

Complete map of Balboa Park shows recreation and picnic areas as well as the cultural zone. Nature trails in Florida Canyon and walking trails on the Park's west side are also shown.

Available at the Balboa Park Visitors Center or online at: **www.ridgwaypark.com**

About the author:

Pam Crooks *retired as Deputy Executive Director for Public Operations at the Reuben H. Fleet Science Center in 1998. Including her time at the Fleet Center, she has been an employee and/or a volunteer in Balboa Park for over 30 years. She's especially proud of helping to develop such collaborative Balboa Park programs as Christmas on the Prado (Balboa Park December Nights), the Passport to Balboa Park and Balboa Park Promotions (Marketing). A long-time board member of the House of Hospitality Association, she served as president of the Association during that historic building's reconstruction in the mid-1990s.*

*Pam continues to volunteer at the Balboa Park Visitor Center on a regular basis and is incoming chair of an advisory board at The San Diego Foundation, which oversees the only significant endowment for Balboa Park: Forever Park (***www.foreverpark.org***). She and husband Ted live right next to the Park and appreciate all that it has to offer on a daily basis.*

About the contributors:

Roger Conlee *is a member and past president of the House of Hospitality Association and a former director of Starlight Musical Theater. Before becoming one of San Diego's most experienced public relations professionals, he was an editor and columnist for the Chicago Daily News, and a reporter and chief copy editor for the San Diego Evening Tribune. His historical novel on the battle of Guadalcanal, "Every Shape, Every Shadow," is available on Amazon.com. One of his favorite things to do in the Park is to spread a blanket and have a summer evening picnic before a performance at the Old Globe or Starlight.*

Mary Anderson *has a special love for Balboa Park that dates back to childhood. Her mother, Elizabeth MacPhail, lawyer, historian and author, wrote many books on San Diego's history including ones on Kate Sessions and Alonzo Horton. Mary began working as a teenager at the Reuben H. Fleet Science Center when it opened in 1973, and continues today, both as part-time console operator in the tilted-dome theater, and as "unofficial" Fleet Center historian. She is also a self-employed real estate appraiser. Naturally, her favorite place in the Park is the Science Center.*

Charlene Baldridge *worked in Balboa Park for many years, first as a volunteer for the San Diego Opera, then as the Old Globe Theatre's Publications and National Media director. Since 1995, she has been a nationally published freelance writer, critic and essayist specializing in the arts. Her favorite places are Palm Canyon and the walkway between the Zoo and Spanish Village.*

Susan Bernstein *worked at the San Diego Museum of Man for 16 years as Education Coordinator. She was involved in many park wide committees including the Balboa Park Educators Council, the Passport to Balboa Park Committee, and the San Diego Inter-Museum Promotion Council. Over the years, Susan became acquainted with almost all the institutions as a museum lover, and has introduced her two children to the Park through camp programs, special events, performances and classes.*

About the House of Hospitality Association:

The non-profit **House of Hospitality Association** *promotes cultural and recreational use of Balboa Park, and is committed to being the primary resource for dissemination of information about the Park. In addition, the Association maintains and preserves its National Historic Landmark building. The three main programs of the House of Hospitality are: the Balboa Park Visitors Center; Balboa Park Marketing; and the official Web site of Balboa Park,* **www.balboapark.org**.